Cricket Witness: No 8

£12.99

A Tale of Three Managers
The Old Hurst Johnian Cricket Week
1920 to 2020

Roger Moulton

First published in Great Britain by
Association of Cricket Statisticians and Historians
Bedford MK40 4FG.
© ACS, 2020

Roger Moulton has asserted his rights under the Copyright, Designs and Patents Act
1988 to be identified as the authors of this work.

British Library Cataloguing-in-Publication Data.
A catalogue record for this book is available from the British Library.

ISBN: 978-1-912421-16-9
Typeset and printed by The City Press Leeds Ltd

Contents

Foreword by Fiona Pitcher

Many Old Hurst Johnians take to being spectators or sometimes scorers after a decade or two – sometimes even three – on the pitch. This writer has been on the boundary or beyond for around half a century, without ever setting foot on the pitch.

This unusual achievement – or failure depending on your perspective – is down to being the grand-daughter of the founder of the Cricket Week who was always rather nervous around cricket balls and also female. Two essential requirements for being a Cricket Week player had not been met.

Despite this challenging start, the Cricket Week has been one of the most enduring parts of my life for which I am very grateful. It started at the tender age of four, courtesy of the generous hospitality of George and Sue Hill and the forbearance, or you could call it determination, of my grandfather, known as "MA" to imbue the delights of a cricket match into his grand-daughter. "MA" incidentally stands for Maurice Albert – two names very much of their time. But we are talking one hundred plus years ago.

Being directly related to the founder brought with it a few privileges. One was to be able to sit next to his array of precision sharp pencils, rulers and records on the upper floor of the Cricket pavilion. This was the equivalent of the VIP area in a nightclub. Few could enter though many tried. So my early years of Cricket Week were spent learning how to score and be very very quiet. Silence had to reign in the pavilion when play was in progress. This was taken very seriously indeed, especially if you were under ten.

Past batting and bowling averages and performances against particular opponents were all there for the reading – and I would sometimes try to memorise these and drop them into the conversation as if an old hand. "MA" also drilled me in the names of Hurst's and its opponents' top cricketers, their personal bests and how they were faring in that day's game. Fielding positions were rather harder to grasp. Silly mid-on is not that useful as a description to someone who has never been on the pitch, never mind standing at silly mid-on.

Scoring was, in hindsight, a very calming, even mindful experience. It requires total concentration and being, as we say now, in the moment. It was only as adolescence and beyond arrived – along with a proper scoreboard away from the pavilion – that the upper floor of the pavilion became a place not for quiet concentration, but for quiet conversation.

With some regret, getting older – or old enough to hold a knife in one hand and a slice of bread in the other – meant that tea-making duties were assigned. This was done by rota and despite all best attempts to avoid it, was, as a non-Cricket playing female, a duty that had to be fulfilled. No such thing as a free tea.

As a young child, Cricket Week off the pitch also consisted of staying "in school", in my case at Martlet House where George Hill was housemaster. This then segued into caravans and tents near Martlet, and then over time to the current "pitch" on Manyweathers overlooking the cricket pitch and pavilion – and the Chapel. A very lovely Sussex view, and a real sense of freedom, especially once riding a bike had been fully mastered. This freedom continues for each new generation that comes to the Cricket Week, and is a special thing.

Off the pitch, there was much fun to be had enjoying the many facilities that the College has to offer – tennis, swimming, and music. Hurst's then music director, Nick Searls, liked to encourage music of all sorts and this included letting me play the Chapel organ. For an 11-year-old this was the equivalent of hosting a set at one of the top music festivals with the best and loudest possible speakers. It was a fantastic opportunity. There were times, I was told rather forcefully by my father – MA's son George – when everyone on the pitch – like it or not – shared the experience. How much the full blast of the Chapel organ was appreciated during play is for others to decide.

Music has always been a tradition at Cricket Week, and still at the end of each Week as the OHJ flag is lowered at the pavilion, Dickie Smart plays The Last Post. Over the years, Hurst has produced some great singers – my Dad George had a good if untrained voice. Informal gatherings to sing everything from Jerusalem to some of the more raucous rugby songs is a tradition that continues. Sam and Tom Moulton keep up the high standards.

By the time I had reached adulthood, my Dad had his Cricket Week caravan, complete with very dodgy fridge and other issues. The camping contingent was growing into a more family-based event which endures to this day. It is a rare thing for three generations to come together for a shared experience, and yet this is part of the Cricket Week tradition. It is even rarer for people to come together every year to spend a week together – for half a century or more. Yet for many, and I am lucky to be one of them, this stays in the diary.

MA, my grandfather, would see a different Cricket Week from the one he began. But thanks to all the players, teachers and families over the years who have continued to support it, it continues to evolve. Oh, and some very good cricket continues to be played.

Fiona Pitcher

Introduction

This book tells the story of the Old Hurst Johnian Cricket Week which has now reached its centenary year. What follows is a tribute to all those who have ever been involved in the Week since that July day in 1920 when the first group of Old Hurst Johnian cricketers arrived to play FE Lander's XI.

It is a remarkable fact that the Week has survived for a hundred years. That this is so is due to a number of factors. Firstly, MA Pitcher, without whose endeavours and boundless enthusiasm we would all be the poorer, developed what was once described as 'an enviable fixture list'. Secondly, the cricket has always been played in the friendly tradition of old boy and wandering cricket without any of the gimmicks of the limited-overs game. Thirdly, the Week has evolved from a bachelor jolly into something in which an entire family can participate. Fourthly, and perhaps most significantly, there have so far only been three managers – MA Pitcher 1920 to 1972, George Hill 1973 to 2004 and Tom Moulton 2005 to the present: hence the title of the book.

Some may feel that old boy and wandering cricket is a world of striped blazers and fancy caps. Perhaps it is, but it is real cricket. A passer-by once asked who was playing. He was told, 'Old Hurst Johnians versus Eton Ramblers.' ' One posh lot against another posh lot,' he observed as he settled down to watch. Having been told that there was a week of matches he became a regular spectator each evening on his way home from work. So, if you have any doubts about this type of cricket, why not come and watch?

This book could not have been written without the help and assistance of a number of people and I am very grateful to them all, especially to George and Sue Hill who sowed the first seeds a few years ago when they asked me when I was going to write the history of the Week. I am only too sorry that Sue did not live to see the finished work.

I must thank Fiona Pitcher not only for writing the Foreword, but also providing all her grandfather's photographs. Archival material is very precious. OHJ cricket is very fortunate that all the Cricket Week scorebooks have survived as have AC Tucker's scrapbooks.

The scorebooks and the reports in the Hurst Johnian and the Hurst Johnian Club Newsletters have been extremely valuable in the writing of this history, but I have absorbed a great deal of information over the last fifty-two years in the many conversations I have had with various Old Hurst Johnian players. I would especially like to mention people who are no longer with us - George Pitcher, Charles Carr, Laurie Henwood and Keith Jenkin. I am greatly indebted to Dick Smart, Willie Welch, Bob Schad, Robin Carr, Roger Goodacre, Jeremy Rawlins, Matt Lowndes, Simon Warrender, Mike Harrison, John Bettridge and finally, the two surviving Managers – George Hill and Tom Moulton - for all their help and encouragement. I am very grateful to Mary-Louise Rowland, the College Archivist, for all her assistance and who has allowed me to quote freely and extensively from the Hurst Johnian and the Hurst Johnian Club Newsletters. Michelle Ashbridge of the Hurst Johnian has also been most helpful.

My thanks also go to Andrew Hignell, editor of the Cricket Witness Series, for overseeing the publication process, Chris Overson and my wife Jenny for their proofreading skills and to all at City Press involved in typesetting and printing.

Roger Moulton
Henfield
March 2020

Chapter One
The First Cricket Week

The report in the October issue of the 1920 *Hurst Johnian* describes what became the first Old Hurst Johnian Cricket Week as 'a venture and an experiment'. On Tuesday 27 July 1920, immediately after the school had broken up for the summer holidays and the Corps had departed for Salisbury Plain, an OHJ team assembled at Hurstpierpoint College to play FE Lander's XI. PW Scott, who combined the roles of Chevron Housemaster and Bursar, had made the Fleur de Lys dormitory and dayroom available for the players so they were able to sleep and feed in the College during the Week.

The first Week did not get off to the most auspicious of starts. 1920 was not one of the better summers of the 20th century and we are told that the team 'arrived in the pouring rain'. The match report went on to say that 'it poured all morning and the prepared pitch was quite impossible.' Nevertheless, a fresh wicket was selected towards the gym end of the square. Even so the match was described as a 'veritable mud splash'.

The OHJ team which took the field in the first match of the first Week consisted of Rev VR Rogers (captain), MA Pitcher, GWE Baker, EL Pitcher, HAH Harris, WH Weller, RO Jenkins, W Smith, RM Esdaile, Rev KG Packard and CW Thomas. The latter two were members of the teaching staff as was Randolph Rogers, an OHJ who had joined the staff as Chaplain after the end of the War.

FE Lander's XI consisted of CE Horser, SJ Langford, I Lorensen, JSB Gentry, FE Lander, WB Ashwell, AE Birch, EW Watts, P Dean, HP Bowden and HJ Ashwell. Very little is known of these players other than that FE Lander had played for a number of teams against the College in previous years and that JSB Gentry represented three first-class counties - Hampshire in 1919, Surrey in 1922 and 1923 and Essex in 1925. Educated at Christ's Hospital where he was in the Eleven for three years, he was a slow bowler who was said to be more effective on dry wickets rather than wet ones.

FE Lander's XI batted first with CE Horser and SJ Langford starting the innings. With the score at 12 MA Pitcher became the first bowler to take a wicket in the Week when he bowled Langford for 12. Horser was joined by Lorensen and the score rose to 126. At that point MA Pitcher and Packard proceeded to run through the rest of Lander's XI who were dismissed for 171 – Packard five for 34 and MA Pitcher five for 86.

The OHJs did not begin well with Gentry (on a wet wicket) dismissing seven of the first eight batsmen at a personal cost of 20 runs. Only Weller with 18 made it into double figures. All out for 61 the first match ended in a defeat by 110 runs. It is interesting to note and is indicative of the way in which cricket was played at that time that at the appointed hour for close of play with the OHJs eight wickets down, it was decided to play on and finish the game so that Lander's XI might win.

Wednesday was another wet day and the match against GE Glenister's XI was curtailed by rain after 27 overs. The scorebook fails to record many of the names of Glenister's team but, as he was the College art master and also very involved in local cricket, especially with both Cuckfield and Hurstpierpoint, this was very likely a team of locals. The names of only ten of the eleven OHJ players are recorded: nine of whom had played the day before and RF Crux, Captain of Cricket in 1915, replacing either Jenkins or Thomas.

The match arranged for Thursday 29 July was supposed to have been against the Sussex Martlets, but in the words of the report in the *Hurst Johnian* they 'let us down badly by scratching at the last moment. However, the energy of two motor cyclists brought an opposition team on to the ground by 11.30.' The assembled group was in effect the Hurstpierpoint village team.

The OHJs batted first and, for the first time, the day was beautifully fine. Nevertheless, the wicket was still soft and all – apart from RF Crux who made 80 – found scoring difficult. The final total of 141 was, however, enough. The Village was dismissed in 23.5 overs for 39. MA Pitcher, with figures of six for 22 and Packard four for 14, bowled unchanged. The Village followed on and were bowled out for 80 with Crux taking five for 23. Thus, the OHJs gained their first Cricket Week victory by an innings and 25 runs.

Friday 30 July saw the final match of the Week which was played on another soft wicket. This time the opposition was mainly drawn from the Royal Engineers Signal Depot at Maresfield with the team titled Lieutenant D Sawer's XI. The OHJs batted first, making 143 with Crux again to the fore with a score of 50. Sawer's XI was dismissed for 118 with MA Pitcher taking six for 40.

Thus, the first Week, consisting of four matches, ended. It appears that there were a number of musicians among the players and that each evening was enlivened with piano, song, recitation and duet. The report in the *Hurst Johnian* concluded that 'the week was voted a great success and ought to become an annual event.'

Chapter Two

The Backgound – a minor public school with a view of the South Downs

The 1920 Old Hurst Johnian Cricket Week had been an obvious success and it established a pattern which has managed to combine tradition with modernity for the last hundred years. The Week survived the disruption caused by the Second War to restart in 1947.

To discover how and why the Week came into being we need to consider the historical background of Hurstpierpoint College and its old pupils' society, the Hurst Johnian Club.

Hurstpierpoint College was founded in 1849 by Nathaniel Woodard who was a curate at St Mary's, Shoreham. He had been influenced by the ideas of the Oxford Movement and, at the same time, had become concerned about the lack of affordable education for the sons and daughters of the middle classes. This led to the foundation of what became Lancing College in 1848, followed a year later by St John's Middle Grammar School in Shoreham. In January 1850 this school moved to Hurstpierpoint where, until suitable accommodation could be built, it was housed in various properties in the village, the most notable of which was the Mansion House. Land was bought to the north and on 21 June 1853 the school moved into its present buildings with views of the South Downs running from Ditchling Beacon in the east to beyond Chanctonbury Ring in the west.

Woodard and Edward Lowe, who was the first Headmaster, obtained a lot of local support for the school. Nathaniel Borrer of Pakyns lent the College fields for playing cricket as did William Campion who opened the nearby grounds of Danny Park to the school for cricket matches. The locals had played here for many years. As early as 1719 Thomas Marchant, a local farmer, recorded in his diary a visit to 'A Cricket Match in ye Sandfield' which is one of several early references to cricket being played in the vicinity of

Hurstpierpoint.

There are no written records of any matches – certainly none has yet come to light – until the appearance of the *Hurst Johnian* in May 1858. This magazine has the distinction of being the oldest continuously published school magazine. From the early cricket reports it can be seen that cricket was well established. The report of the match between the school and the Old Hurst Johnians in 1858 – or Past v Present as it was called for many years – gives every indication that cricket at Hurst already had a solid history.

Matches were played against local sides such as Hurstpierpoint, Ditchling and Burgess Hill. The first inter-school match appears to have been one played against Woodard's newly founded Ardingly College in 1859. Lancing College was first played in 1863.

The major problem was the lack of a suitable ground. In 1861 part of the West Field (now built over) was used for cricket, but it was very rough and uneven, requiring much rolling which was done by the boys. In February 1863 there was a fatal accident: the heavy horse roller was being pulled by a group of boys when John Clothier slipped and 'the heavy instrument passed over the poor boy who never spoke again.'

It was not until 1864 that the present ground – the North Field – came into use. This was developed from two fields on the north side of the school which had been bought in 1861. The boys grubbed up the hedge between the two fields and, although the ground was in action three years later, it took many years of effort before it reached the perfection of today. A pavilion was built in 1888 and stood until 1921 when it was replaced by the present structure.

Although specifically aimed at sons of the middle classes, Hurstpierpoint College always regarded itself, and was regarded by others, as a public school. In the later years of the nineteenth century it played the MCC, had an old boys' club, an Officer Training Corps, played cricket and football matches against other public schools, published its averages in *Lillywhite* and *Wisden* and had details of its matches in *Scores and Biographies*. The College had a long-running school magazine – the *Hurst Johnian* – and was mentioned in the *Public Schools* magazine as well as having a host of public school traditions.

Unfortunately, it has to be said that the standard of Hurst cricket was not always very high. When Hurst beat Lancing in 1890 it was the first time since 1878 and the *Hurst Johnian* described the homecoming of the triumphant team in these terms:

> So the charm was broken and the non-success which has attended our efforts since 1878 was dispelled. Boundless as was the delight of the Eleven, it was nothing compared to the joy at home which was ecstatic and frenzied. After Evensong the entire School, headed by all the masters, went down the road, past the icehouse to meet the Eleven. There they lined up and waited for the team, whose choruses could be heard afar off as they came up the road. When they got there, Pandemonium was let loose, and with cheers, yells, shrieks, hysteric sobs, voiceless gesticulations, the blare of trumpets, and the bray of trombones, night was made hideous for the ten minutes occupied in getting back to college. Smith and Keeling were carried shoulder high and "God save the Queen" was sung in a way that accounts for the voiceless state of the choir next morning. Altogether a night to be much remembered and may it be repeated!

Performances against MCC were not always covered in glory. In 1888, before declarations were permitted, MCC batted all day, reaching a total of 577 for 8. This was not the only occasion that Hurst bowling was put to the sword. Nor did the College always redeem itself with the bat. That said, up to 1914, a number of boys went on to play first-class cricket.

FFJ Greenfield captained both Cambridge University and Sussex. AJ Sharood and JP Anscombe also played for Sussex. WG Heasman, a friend of KS Ranjitsinjhi, appeared for Sussex as well as for Berkshire and Norfolk. AR Layman and HW Keeling played for Kent as did WL Knowles who later became the Sussex Secretary. R Turner, a Cambridge soccer blue, appeared for Gloucestershire. CT Stuart snr played for Natal and is the only OHJ to have umpired a first-class match. HE Moffatt kept wicket in the Oxford University Freshmen's match of 1898. J Horstead played for Canada. RSK Blucke (Dorset), AJ Chivers (Wiltshire), VR Rogers (also Wiltshire) and HM and JS Harford (both Hertfordshire) all played Minor County Cricket. William Pratt, old boy and master from 1853 to 1906, was famous for bowling WG Grace when he had made his first century – 170 for South Wales against the Gentlemen of Sussex on the Royal Brunswick Ground, Hove in 1864. J Swart was one of the founder members of the Wanderers Club in Johannesburg.

The problem with Hurst cricket was probably not so much the lack of talent but that few masters stayed for any length of time and that no first-class cricketer joined the staff until PA Gibb did so in 1938; and sadly it has to be recorded that schoolmastering was not his forte. A lack of coaches also meant that all was concentrated on the 1st XI. There was a handful of 2nd XI and Under 15 XI matches, but today's ladder of progression through the age groups was virtually non-existent. Nor did the fact that masters played in matches against clubs until 1893 do much for team building. Examination of scorecards shows that more or less every 1st XI carried players who batted unsuccessfully down the order and never bowled. The small size of the school did not help either. Nor did the fact that many boys left early which made for a small VI form.

Nevertheless, there were some successful teams and there were usually some good players. In fact, in terms of inter-school matches in the period up to and including 1914, 189 matches were played against other schools of which 89 were won, 16 drawn, 83 lost and 1 tied, but the fixture list also contained matches against clubs. In 1914, for example, Hurst played Lancing, Ardingly, Cranleigh, Whitgift and City of London – all of which could be reached by train – as well as The Masters, Hurstpierpoint Cricket Club, MCC,

OHJs, Sutton, the Dolphins, St Mary's, A Gorham's XI and AR Layman's XI. Both Gorham and Layman were old boys of the College.

Although playing standards may not have reached the highest levels and were rather modest when compared to schools of a similar age, there was obviously much enthusiasm for the game. Especially was this so with the generation who were in the school in the years just before the war and it is significant that in 1919 the OHJs were able to put out a 1st XI and a 2nd XI to play the College on Whit Monday and that this continued until 1957 when the 2nd XI fixture finally disappeared. There were occasions too when a 3rd XI took the field. The fixture was an important occasion in the Summer Term and one can see how the idea of a Cricket Week would have germinated. There had, however, to be a driving force behind it.

That driving force was Maurice Pitcher, known to all as MA. With his brother EL, he had arrived, aged 13, at Hurst in September 1911 and had joined Fleur de Lys whose Housemaster was HM Parham. He was one of eighteen boys who arrived at the College that term, four of whom were to lose their lives in the Great War. MA was a member of the 1st XI in 1913 and 1914, being awarded his 1st XI colours in the latter season. The report in the *Hurst Johnian* described him as 'a bowler of unusual action who has several times been useful'. He was a good soccer player who was, we are told, 'an unobtrusive, but most useful half; is a good tackler and reliable in defence:' he was in the Ist XI for two seasons. He left Hurst in March 1915 and was later commissioned in the Dorset Regiment.

MA did not appear for the OHJ XI in the match against the College in 1919, but he made his mark in the 1920 match with an innings of 69. The following day he assisted AR Layman's XI against the College, scoring 39. One assumes that it was during or just after these two matches that plans were made for a cricket week after the end of the Summer Term with MA making all the arrangements.

Chapter Three

MA Pitcher Part 1: 1920 to 1939

In the summer of 1921 the College completed its memorials to the 108 old boys and masters who had been killed during the Great War. The names are recorded on a panel in the Memorial Chapel. The panel behind the altar, the credence table, the stalls and gates are also memorials. There was some money left over and it was decided to use the bulk of it to build a new pavilion in place of the one erected in 1888. Work began in January 1921 and on 23 July the building, designed by John Hunt, an OHJ, was opened by Major-General Sir John Steevens, who had been in the 1st XI from 1869 to 1871. A match was played between the College and what was described as an OJ Service team. The College batted first and made 159 with A Goodger of the 1914 XI taking five for 49 and MA four for 46. In reply the Service team made 115 thus losing by 44 runs. MA was second highest scorer with 24.

Although the drainage and lavatory arrangements were still incomplete, the pavilion was in use during the Week of 1921 which had been moved to the first week of August, with the first match taking place on the Bank Holiday Monday. This year there were five matches, two of which were against scratch sides – HS Mills' XI and RO Jenkins' XI. The third opponent was an XI from Maresfield Camp, an Army base on the edge of Maresfield. This was not as unusual as it might seem as the College 1st XI had played them on a number of occasions in previous seasons.

The two remaining opponents were the Old Brightonians and the Old Colfeians. The Old Brightonian fixture lasted for three years and has never been revived. The Old Colfeian match lasted until 1934 with home and away games being played in 1925.

1921 was the seventh best summer of the 20th century and at this point only 1911 had been better. The Week itself was described as 'a gorgeous success in every way'. Four matches were won. HS Mills' XI was defeated by 170 runs in a match distinguished by an opening partnership of 137 runs made by WDC Keeson, who made 94, and EL Pitcher. The next match, against Maresfield Camp, was lost by 40 runs. The third match was against the Old Brightonians who, despite the presence in their ranks of AJ Murdoch-Cozens who played in four matches for Sussex, were dismissed for 85 with MA taking six for 10. The Old Colfeians were defeated by three wickets who, having set the OHJs 150 to win, very sportingly extended the time for drawing stumps. RO Jenkins's XI was beaten by an innings and 47 runs with A Goodger taking six for 14.

Socially the Week was clearly a great success. We are told that:

> the cricket by no means exhausted the potentialities of the team. It contained a really good pianist, vocalists of every degree of excellence, a most accomplished reciter and a black and white artist whose pictures would add lustre to the pages of *Punch*.

The artist was AC Tucker. It is thanks to him that the club has an extensive collection of sketches of both players and incidents in the years up to 1939. He was not what would have been described as a great cricketer, but he was always ready to play when needed or when the opposition was unable to raise a complete team. In the war he had served in Palestine and his sketch book of that campaign is with the Imperial War Museum.

It should also be recorded that the Headmaster, Canon AH Coombes, became the first and only Headmaster to take an active part in the Week, umpiring in all five matches. He had been a cricketer of repute at Magdalen College School, Oxford. Cricket Archive records only one match in which he appeared. This was against Bloxham School in 1880. He scored 10 and 17 and took six for 21 and eight for 23 in a victory for Magdalen College School. Until Canon Bruce Ruddock began umpiring in 2018 he was the only Canon of the Church of England to umpire in Cricket Week.

By the autumn of 1921 money for the pavilion had run out, and so the drainage arrangements were completed by the boys in the College who remarkably did all the necessary work in three days without, of course, being paid. Adorned by a clock in memory of the four masters who had been killed in the war, one of whom was Richard Willis who had been master in charge of cricket in 1913 and 1914, the pavilion is still in use today and is very largely unchanged. Situated in the south-west corner of the North Field, it may be seen from all parts of the Field.

The 1922 Week began with a match against the Old Colfeians who won comfortably, thanks to the bowling of P Rees who took seven for 18 and nine for 37 as the OHJs slid to defeat by 80 runs. HS Mills' XI was defeated by 112 runs. The main feature of this match was the scoring of the first Cricket Week century. Hitting three 6s and eight 4s, DR Baylis made 102*, nearly half of the OHJ score of 218 for 7 declared.

Then followed a two-day match against the Old Brightonians who won by an innings and 115 runs. Thanks to the bowling of AK Wilson – a Sussex player and later County Club chairman – who took seven for 27, the OHJs were dismissed for 83. The Old Brightonians made 249. The writer of the match report was very critical of the OHJ fielding:

> The fielding of the O.Js. was deplorable. After the first one or two missed catches the infection spread rapidly and hardly a member of the team came off the field with an untarnished record.

After this display in the field there was a batting collapse, the OHJs being all out for 51. Corbett took six for 20 and AK Wilson acquired another four wickets giving him match figures of 13 for 48.

The final match was the first one against the Sussex Martlets. The OHJs made 175 and had reduced the Martlets to 46 for 5 when rain at about 5.15 pm brought the match to an end. With what was described as 'excellent length bowling,' GE Crosbie had taken five for 16 in 12 overs. The

Sussex Martlets fixture endures to this day.

The writer of the Cricket Week report, whom we may assume to have been MA Pitcher, was somewhat critical:

> But for the sake of the School's reputation we could wish that the cricket had reached a higher standard. There is all the difference in the world between being beaten after a good fight, and never looking as if one could win: and in two of the matches played the latter was certainly the impression conveyed. It seems to us that the net should be thrown somewhat wider in future years and that every effort should be made to get our more distinguished cricketers to come down if only for one match or two. There will always be a good many who will come for the sake of the Week's reunion without caring whether they play in every match; and these could be retained while the sterner business of winning the matches be entrusted to real experts.

It will have been noticed by the observant reader that there were a number of matches against what may be described as scratch teams. At this point OHJ cricket was not well-established. It is true that the first recorded match against the School was played in 1858 and that there is clear evidence that this was already an established fixture, but no other matches appear to have been played apart from five games between 1895 and 1901 against Bushey, with which there were strong OHJ connections, and one against the City of London School in 1914. It was clearly going to take time to develop and maintain a fixture list and to sell the idea of the Cricket Week to a greater number of old boys.

That these problems have been solved is down to the efforts of the three men who have managed the Week – Maurice Pitcher 1920 to 1972, George Hill 1973 to 2004 and Tom Moulton from 2005 to the present. Between them they all managed to recruit a continual stream of players and maintain the development of the fixture list.

The fixture pattern for the inter-war period is unlike that of the present day. Since 1971 the only newcomer to the list has been the South Wales Hunts who replaced the Free Foresters in 1991 who then returned in 2019 when Romany dropped out after 63 years. Such continuity, which is remarkable in the current climate of wandering and old boys' cricket, was clearly not the case in the 1920/39 period where 26 different sides were played. Of these, 11 might be described as scratch sides, got up to fill a gap in the fixture list. Two of them – WM Bradley's XI and W. Riches' XI – appeared regularly at Hurst playing both the school and the old boys. Another regular visitor was the Rev CH Clarke's XI which seems mostly to have been composed of local clergy. Clarke himself was an active cricketer making many appearances for the Sussex Martlets. Gradually the scratch elevens made way for club sides such as Hove (1924 to 1930), Kingston (1926 to 1929) and Hampton Wick (1931 to 1954).

After their failure to produce a team in 1920 the Sussex Martlets have appeared every season since 1922 – a total of 89 matches of which two were cancelled because of rain.

Other long-standing opponents to appear before the war were Leicester Ivanhoe who ran a southern tour every August. The fixture ran from 1933 to 1937 and was then revived in 1948 lasting until 1968. The Stoics, who had played the school from 1882 to 1913, first appeared in the Week in 1935 and have been regulars ever since. Matches were played against Romany in 1937 and 1938 who subsequently replaced Hampton Wick in 1955, continuing until 2018. Another interesting fixture was one against RAF Cranwell which took place in 1938 and 1939, but which was not renewed after the war.

Against this background of a developing fixture list – entirely due to the zeal and enthusiasm of MA Pitcher – a standard pattern evolved. The Week began on the Bank Holiday Monday and five matches were played with everyone departing after Friday's match. It was extended to the Saturday in 1948, with a Sunday match being added at the beginning of the Week in 1955. The Saturday start began in 1965, thus extending the Week to eight days which continues to the present day.

It was a bachelor week with the majority of the players staying in the College. The Bursar in 1920 was PW Scott, a man who devoted his life to Hurstpierpoint College. He had arrived in September 1901 as a temporary master. His ability was immediately apparent and within weeks he became a permanent member of the staff. One of the last acts of the Headmaster, Rev CE Cooper, was to make him Housemaster of Chevron in March 1902, a post which he held until his retirement in 1950. In 1920 Scott took over the role of Bursar and, as if this was not enough, he became Second Master in 1931. The mind boggles at the thought of anyone being able to combine the roles of Housemaster, Second Master and Bursar in today's complex and highly regulated educational world.

Scott was a great supporter of the Week and is to be found in many group photographs. He was a regular visitor to the Week after he had retired to Bognor. He always made a dormitory available and arranged for food to be provided. In addition to MA Pitcher, another driving force behind the early Weeks was Rev VR Rogers. Randolph Rogers was an OHJ (1898-1904) and was a good enough cricketer to have played for Wiltshire in Minor Counties cricket. Ordained before the war he served as an Army Chaplain before volunteering for active service. In 1919 he returned to Hurst becoming Chaplain. He lived with his beautiful wife in Ruckford House – just across Malthouse Lane which is the eastern boundary of the North Field. We are informed that the players gathered regularly in the evenings at Ruckford House with EL Pitcher to the fore with his piano playing.

Other members of staff soon became involved both on and off the field – Rev KG Packard, CW Thomas, HBI Pocock and HM Parham all appear in group photographs. Staff and former staff involvement continues to this day which helps to promote the very strong links between OHJ cricket and the College.

A problem for any cricket club – whatever its playing

standard might be – is the recruitment and retention of players. This is often difficult for a town or village club which can in theory draw from the locality, but the Old Hurst Johnians were handicapped in other ways. Firstly, the College was a boarding school, recruiting pupils not only from the whole of Sussex but also from overseas. Secondly, it was a small school. The OHJ players of the pre-war period had all been members of a school whose numbers averaged around 150. Thirdly, and this has always been the case, staying for the entire Week meant giving up a week's holiday.

Thus the player pool was small, and not all positions – batting, bowling and fielding – could be filled adequately. We are told that in 1923 the presence of Nicholson, Weller and Pring added considerably to the strength of the batting, but that the bowling lacked variety – there were three quick bowlers but a reliable slow bowler was needed. In 1924 there were eight wicketkeepers available!

There was, however, a hard core of players who came every year without fail and this has been the case ever since. By 1939, 79 players had appeared in the Week. Of these MA Pitcher had played in all 20 Weeks, closely followed by AC Tucker 19, WH Weller 17, DG Jeffery 15, CI'A Carr 13 and DG Mills 12. The average number of players in each Week hovered around 15. Use was made of masters, such as Rev KG Packard, CW Thomas, and HBI Pocock. Members of the teaching staff are regarded as members of the Hurst Johnian Club. More recently the qualification for playing has been extended to sons of OHJs.

The Week of 1923 was considered to be a big improvement on that of 1922. The weather was perfect and it was felt that the wickets were almost too good. Both batting and bowling were stronger than that produced the year before, although MA stated that the presence of a slow bowler would have helped.

The Old Colfeians were defeated by 131 runs. Rogers (55) and Nicholson (96) put on 117 for the first wicket. The game against the Sussex Martlets ended in a draw. The two-day match against the Old Brightonians was notable for AK Wilson's great performance. In the first OHJ innings he took seven for 52 and followed this in the second innings with ten for 87, giving him match figures of seventeen for 139. Wilson's ten for 87 remained the best bowling performance in the Week until Stuart Rankin took ten for 31 for the Buccaners in 1973. Strangely the *Hurst Johnian* match report makes no mention of Wilson's all ten. Nor did anyone seem to notice that he had taken 28 OHJ wickets in two seasons.

The next day Rogers hit up 127 out of a total of 363 to give the OHJs a 213 run victory over CW Mills' XI. Incisive bowling by Crux with four for 21, and MA Pitcher, five for 45, led to a heavy defeat of GM Jeffery's XI to end the Week on a high note. The 1923 Week saw two appearances of note: FRS Whitbourn (Star 1891/97) who became the only entirely nineteenth century OHJ to play in the Week and Denis Jeffery, a power in the land until his death in June 1972.

1924 was a wet summer with soft wickets and, although the weather during the Week was deemed unpleasant, there was little interference with the actual cricket. We are told that the wicket for the Old Colfeian game was 'soft... absolutely dead on account of the heavy rain which fell during Sunday evening.' The OHJs won by 35 runs. On another slow wicket the Sussex Martlets were victorious by 23 runs.

There were three new fixtures – Sussex Clergy which ended in a draw 'although the weather was all that could be required, the bowlers received no help from the pitch'. Thirteen of the twenty-two players were clergymen – eleven Sussex Clergy and Rogers and Cartridge for the OHJs. Chichester Priory were beaten by 106 runs in their only match against the OHJs. Weller made 76 out of a total of 147. Chichester Priory folded for 41 – Rogers taking six for 26 and Goodger three for 14. In another new fixture Hove were defeated by 26 runs, thanks to 41 from Weller and then six for 35 from Rogers and four for 36 from

Goodger. As has already been mentioned this was the year of the eight wicketkeepers although the work was actually shared by Mills, who had played for Surrey Young Amateurs against Surrey Young Professionals in 1919, and Gillis.

Again in 1925 the weather was poor. The wickets were soft and rain spoiled two matches. It was clearly yet another sociable Week. Of the 16 who played eleven were there for the entire time.

The Week got off to a good start with a 107-run victory over the Old Colfeians which made up for the defeat at Lee two weeks earlier. On that occasion the OHJs, batting first, had collapsed to 53 for 9 when Denis Jeffery joined EL Pitcher who had opened the batting. Together they had added 73 for the last wicket when Jeffery was dismissed for 52. Well known for his strong and resolute defence, EL was unbeaten on 37. The Cricket Week match – a 12-a-side game – was dominated by Randolph Rogers, who carried his bat for 97, and VG Curnow, who took five for 60 as the OHJS reached 217. The Old Colfeians got off to a bad start losing three wickets for six runs and were beaten by 110 runs, Denis Jeffery finishing with six for 51. The Sussex Martlets were defeated by 30 runs, although the reporter in the *Hurst Johnian* felt that the match might have gone either way.

Rain delayed the start of the match against the Sussex Clergy, five of whom did not bother to turn up. Substitutes – including CW Thomas – were eventually found and the match started at 2.30 pm ending in a comfortable OHJ victory, thanks to a partnership of 120 between VJ Grinsted, 91, and AF Gillis, 46.

The Chichester Priory match was replaced by one against RJ Coley's XII which was ended by rain after 90 minutes' play. Hove were defeated by 52 runs. Sadly this turned out to be Randolph Rogers' last match. He failed to score but took four for 21. Taken ill in October, he died on 6 November aged only 40. His widow continued to live in Ruckford House for many years.

1926 was yet another wet summer. The Australian tourists had many matches ruined by the rain, notably the First Test at Trent Bridge which was abandoned after England had reached 32-0 in 17 overs. It was, however, very different at Hurst. The Week 'turned out brilliantly fine.' Twenty players were available and only the last match was rain-affected. The report gives a flavour of the social side of the Week:

> We missed "Grandad" Whitbourn from the dormitory, though we had his cheery company on the ground each day, and we also missed EL Pitcher, whose music has been for many years a feature of our evening's entertainment. Still the younger generation found consolation in Gilbert and Sullivan and the Oxford Song Book. To Mrs Rogers, for her kind hospitality each evening we wish to express our grateful thanks.

The Old Colfeian match was a high-scoring draw with 137.5 overs being bowled in the day. The OHJs made 285 (Curnow seven for 66) and the match ended in a draw with the Old Colfeians on 218 for 6. The Sussex Clergy, aided by DG Mills and CR Gerrard, were defeated by 179 runs. Gerrard, later a member of the Sussex committee, was the Clergy's best bowler with two for 60. G Smith scored 142 – the highest score in the Week thus far. The Clergy collapsed for 122 – Mills and Gerrard making 48 of them – and EE Pring (one of five brothers) taking four for 19. The Sussex Martlets had HR Munt (later a prominent member of Sir Julien Cahn's XI) in their ranks. He took four for 34 in an OHJ innings of 168. Cartridge made 81 but it was not enough to prevent a Martlet victory.

Once again there was a new fixture – this time with Kingston and it ended in an OHJ victory. As already mentioned the match against Hove ended with the rain falling, but not before MA had taken five for 49 and Gerrard four for 55. Charles Carr's Cricket Week career began this year. He played regularly until 1959 and, as we shall see, became the first President of the Duck Club. After his playing days were over he ran the bar in the pavilion with a firm and genial manner.

The 1927 Week turned out to be another good one, although for the most part it was once more a wet summer. The reporter in the *Hurst Johnian* was especially critical of the fielding as lacking 'the keenness to which we have become accustomed, and at times was even slovenly.' The bowling was described as 'weak' and 'limited'. He also expressed the wish that more Old Boys would come:

> Of course, the cricket is the important thing... but we should like to stress the social side – the reunion of O.Js., the exchange of reminiscences, the joys(?) of sleeping once again in a dorm on a bed with wonky springs and a knobbly mattress – we feel that there must be numbers of O.J.s who would enjoy coming. And there are tennis and fives, and two golf courses within easy reach: so there are other attractions besides the cricket.

This was the Week which saw the first appearance of one of the great stalwarts of OHJ cricket – Jack Youngman, a stickler for etiquette of the game who, blessed with a fantastic eye, played off the front foot with superb timing. Rain ruined the Old Colfeian match when the OHJs had reached 106 for 1. The Sussex Clergy disappeared from the fixture list and were replaced by the the Rev'd CH Clarke's XI which, containing nine parsons, lost by 102 runs after Weller had made 136 in an OHJ total of 240. There was a 12-a-side match against the Sussex Martlets who had little trouble in winning by four wickets. Kingston were defeated by 76 runs with Denis Jeffery to the fore with five for 42 in 27.1 overs. In the OHJ reply Jack Youngman displayed his class with an innings of 81.

The Hove match was described as 'a disastrous game'. The match was dominated by the 19 year-old HE Hammond who was to play 196 matches for Sussex as well as being a noted inside forward with Fulham. He opened the batting for Hove, making 117 (the first opposition century in the Week), before being stumped by AF Gillis off the bowling of Cartridge. All out for 307, Hove then dismissed the OHJs for 99, of which Cartridge made 59, Hammond taking six for 38.

The final match was played at Lancing. This game, which ended in a draw appears to have been the only fixture between the OHJS and Lancing Rovers until the two clubs met in the Cricketer Trophy in 2015.

The reporter in the *Hurst Johnian* was much happier in 1928. The opening paragraph of the report is almost ecstatic:

> Another week has come and gone, a week full of good things, an increased fixture list; two records, a highest score, and a highest individual aggregate; some excellent batting; some hurricane hitting by the skipper; some good bowling; three really exciting finishes, five perfect pitches and one that was not; glorious sunshine: what more could one wish for?

Charles Carr made 327 runs in the Week and LR Dixon scored 300 runs in four innings. It should also be noted that 1928 was the best summer since the Week started in 1920. Seventeen players appeared in the six matches but the *Hurst Johnian* reporter was left wanting more:

> Again we could wish that more O.J.s would join us during the Week on the principle of 'the more the merrier' yet we can look back to a very enjoyable time, and look forward to happy reunions in future years.

The Old Colfeians made 246 (Denis Jeffery bowling 28 overs to take four for 58) but the OHJs could only manage 192 with VG Curnow to the fore once again taking six for 28. The next match was against the Rev CH Clarke's XI who made 185. In their ranks was RdeWK Winlaw, who later played for Cambridge University and Surrey, top-scoring with 74, but the rest of the team was unable to cope with JFA Campbell who took nine for 52 in 25.1 overs. He had taken the first eight wickets when CW Thomas dismissed the eighth batsman thereby depriving him of the possibility of all ten. In keeping with the times the OHJs batted until the close of play reaching the record total of 370 for 4 off 51.2 overs – Dixon 127, Nicholson 86, Carr 66, MA Pitcher

43*. It is recorded that MA only batted for 12 minutes. The match against the Sussex Martlets ended in a draw and Kingston won by two wickets. This game was described as being one of 'fluctuating fortunes'. The OHJs reached 231 thanks to 100 from Dixon. Kingston's reply fluctuated from 74 for 1 to 128 for 7, then 194 for 8 before winning by 2 wickets. This year – HE Hammond was unavailable as he was now on the Sussex staff – the Hove match was drawn. Carr made the first century of his career, making 121. His innings was described as 'a real good effort'. The OHJs reached 312 but Hove held out for a draw with nine down for 229.

The last game was against Haywards Heath and was played away. Haywards Heath made 117 with Campbell taking six for 33. Unfortunately the OHJs lost by 2 runs. Only Charles Carr, who made 32, 'faced the bowling with confidence'. The pitch was described as 'decidedly sporting, the ball getting up dangerously at times, while shooters were not unknown.'

In terms of results 1929 was highly successful. R Lee, LG Garnett, DG Jeffery and JFA Campbell were a formidable quartet of bowlers who kept opponents' scores to modest totals. Unfortunately the batting was not as effective – Dixon was missing and Carr was not the force of 1928. Three matches were won – Old Colfeians, against whom Garnett made 105, Hove and Haywards Heath. Rain washed out the game against the Rev CH Clarke's XI and the Sussex Martlets match was left unfinished. Kingston were played for the last time. This was a low-scoring match which ended in a Kingston win. The Hove game finished in an OHJ victory after the OHJs batting first had been 28 for 5 and then 49 for 6. MA then rode to the rescue with a whirlwind 60 made in half an hour. Hove needed 158 but collapsed to 99 all out. The Week finished with an excellent win against Haywards Heath. On a wicket described as 'none too good' the OHJs reached 111. Haywards Heath were dismissed for 33 – Lee four for 16 and Campbell six for 17. Following on Haywards Heath managed 33 with Lee taking seven for 12.

1930 was considerably rain-affected. The match against the Old Colfeians started on a dead wicket which then gradually dried out. After declaring on 158 for 6 the Old Colfeians dismissed the OHJs for 75, Hithersay taking five for 32. There was then further rain and the next match against Rev CH Clarke's XI was played on a new wicket cut at the gym end of the North Field, but more rain ended the match after 15 overs had been bowled.

The next match was against the Sussex Martlets who were beaten for the first time since the Week had started. There was further interference from the rain and the next match – a new one against WM Bradley's XI – was played on the far side of the North Field. The rain then relented for the last match of the Week which was against Hove. This was definitely Lee's match. He made 101 out of an OHJ total of 242 before taking seven for 52 to reduce Hove to 193 for 9 although the game was drawn. This turned out to be the last OHJ match against Hove.

As far as first-class cricket is concerned 1931 was the worst summer since 1912, not being surpassed until 1954. It therefore comes as a surprise to read in the *Hurst Johnian* that:

> In contrast to the last season, this year we were favoured with glorious weather. On two days, Tuesday and Wednesday, ominous clouds rolled up about tea-time, lightning flashed, and thunder crashed, but though copious rain fell within a few miles of the College, hardly a spot reached the North Field, and games were not even interrupted.

Several stalwarts of previous Weeks were missing. Jeffery and Campbell carried the bowling. Between them they bowled 218 overs while the remaining bowlers sent down a mere 70. No one scored many runs and, perhaps not surprisingly, for the first time no matches were won.

There were some noteworthy performances. Jeffery took five for 49 against the Old Colfeians in a match where each side batted twice with SL Goatly making a pair. Jeffery then took six for 62 against the Rev CH Clarke's XI. Dixon top-scored with 121 against the Sussex Martlets. The Hove fixture was replaced with one against Hampton Wick from Middlesex which thus began a series of matches which lasted until 1954. In a high-scoring game the OHJs made 288 and Hampton Wick were 12 runs short of victory with two wickets in hand. Playing for Hampton Wick was JEdeW Denning who made 95 and took five for 51. Denning, an Old Hurst Johnian, had been Captain of Cricket in 1905, 1906 and 1907. Playing most of his cricket for Ealing, he is one of the few club cricketers – Jack Youngman was another at that level – to have made a hundred hundreds. He also represented Buckinghamshire in the Minor Counties Championship. It was always a matter of regret that he rarely played any OHJ cricket.

In 1932 the weather was fine, but heavy rain in the preceding week led to rather soft wickets. Player recruitment was a problem and the only victory was over the Rev CH Clarke's XI which was making its last appearance in the Week. The matches against the Old Colfeians, Sussex Martlets, WM Bradley's XI and Hampton Wick all ended in defeat.

Of these games, that against the Sussex Martlets was the most exciting. The Martlets scored 178 with PH Riseley taking five for 70. Needing 179 to win the OHJs collapsed to 44 for 5. EJ Riseley and Bradbrooke then added 110 for the sixth wicket. Finally, with one wicket remaining, Rawkins was joined by PH Riseley. The report continues:

> A two, a six and then another big hit. Everybody cheering and the batsman watching the ball as it goes towards the boundary. The lofted ball was stopped – it isn't a four. The batsmen scramble two. Still two runs are wanted. Over is called. Rawkins pushes the first ball he receives gently towards mid-on and calls. Riseley is a bit late in responding and the game is over.

WFT O'Byrne, who played one match for Sussex in 1935 and was a regular member of the Sussex Second XI, took five for 53 for the Martlets.

Elsewhere in the *Hurst Johnian* it was reported that Jack Youngman, last seen in the 1927 Week, had scored 1428

runs for the Westminster Bank with a highest score of 145*
and an average of 52.80.

It was very different in 1933. The reporter was in happier
vein:

> Cricket weeks come and go, but few cricket weeks can
> have provided such good sport as this year's matches
> have. One match was lost by five runs, two others
> were won after all had seemed lost, while in another
> a formidable score of 343 was awarded by the third
> century being reached before the third wicket fell.
> Though rain did fall on Friday, it did not interrupt
> the game for long; on the other days the sun shone
> and conditions for spectators and players alike were
> delightful.

The match against the Old Colfeians was lost, but the
presence of two much younger OHJs – C Mertens and HS
Deighton – was noted with pleasure. 1933 saw the first
visit of Leicester Ivanhoe who, despite the presence of two
first-class players – EA Broughton and AG Weston – in their
ranks, were dismissed for 156 (Jeffery six for 46). Batting
on, as was then customary, the OHJs responded with a
total of 261.

Once again there was a close finish to the Sussex Martlets
game – defeat by 5 runs. The match against WM Bradley's
XI produced a match aggregate of 657. The visitors made
343 of which AE Jones made 132, reaching his hundred
before lunch and going on to make what was then the
highest score against an OHJ side. The story goes that the
captain of WM Bradley's XI decided not to declare because
he had spotted that Jack Youngman was playing. The OHJs
began their response and Carr was soon out, but

> Youngman and Carrington carried the score to 57,
> Youngman playing very confidently and doing most
> of the scoring and later Weller helped in a stand
> which carried the score to 140 for 4. Jeffery then
> joined Youngman, and curbing his natural game very
> considerably, he was content to leave most of the
> scoring to Youngman and the two, by cricket which was

most attractive to watch, pushed the score along until it reached 300. Then Jeffery, who had just completed his half century, was caught, and Pitcher decided to go for the runs. There were 40 to be made in ten minutes, a difficult task against bowling which, in spite of the number of runs made against it, had never got loose. Both Bradbrooke and Pitcher failed through trying to hit, and after another 14 runs had been added, stumps were drawn, with the total 314 for seven. Youngman's 191 not out was a wonderful effort. He gave no chance and his thity-three 4s signify the strength of his driving. The score is a record for O.J.Week, and also constitutes a personal record. Congratulations, Youngman!

This OHJ record still stands and only two visiting players have ever surpassed it – T McCall with 242* for the Eton Ramblers in 2012 and SP Cooper who made 205* for the Sussex Martlets in 2015.

After all these excitements the Week ended with a 20-run win over Hampton Wick. The OHJs made 157. In reply Hampton Wick were 96 for 0 before being all out for 137 against the bowling of Lattimer who took seven for 33.

After scoring 282 runs in four matches in 1933 Jack Youngman did not reappear in 1934. In fact he did not return until 1949. Charles Carr scored 233 runs in the five games, but no bowler got near 20 wickets and the fielding was described as 'hardly up to standard', and, as a result, no matches were won. There were, however, several newcomers, two of whom – Leo Ricketts and Bill Coley – were destined to play highly significant roles in the future running of the Week.

The 1934 Week saw the last visit of the Old Colfeians who won the match without much difficulty. The Leicester Ivanhoe game ended in defeat. There was a draw against the Sussex Martlets before WM Bradley's XI was again successful. Rain ruined the Hampton Wick game but not before the Somerset player AES Rippon had reached 62. Rippon was one of a pair of twins who played for Somerset and was the father of Geoffrey Rippon, a prominent member of Margaret Thatcher's Cabinets. This year a sixth game was played. This was against the Old Ardinians and was played at Ardingly College. The OHJs were defeated, but Carr and Weller batted well and MA Pitcher took eight for 65.

1935 was a good summer and the Week 'was favoured with brilliant sunshine'. It was felt that the batting was weaker than usual. Denis Jeffery was the leading bowler – 27 wickets in 104 overs at a cost of 12.30. The next best bowler was Campbell whose 11 wickets cost 29.90 apiece. The highest run scorer was Rawkins who scored 138 at an average of 23.00. Sixteen players appeared in the Week. Of these eight played in all six matches. It was indeed a small group which kept the Week going.

The Old Colfeians were replaced by the Stoics who had played the College from 1882 to 1913. It was not an auspicious return to Hurst as they were defeated by 103 runs, largely thanks to Campbell's six for 41.

Leicester Ivanhoe produced a very strong team containing four first-class players, one of whom was the New Zealand Test player CS Dempster, who is recognized as one of the greatest of all New Zealand batsmen. He had taken a post with the furniture magnate Sir Julien Cahn who ran his own cricket team and who was a patron of Leicestershire and Nottinghamshire cricket. In 1935 Dempster was completing his three year qualification period for Leicestershire, hence his availability for Leicester Ivanhoe. In the event Dempster batted stolidly and was caught by Bradbrooke off the bowling of Lattimer for 25. AP Thompson then made an unbeaten 140 and Leicester Ivanhoe declared at 261 for 9 before proceeding to bundle out the OHJs for 76. The report concluded:

> About the O.J. innings, the less said the better: only Pitcher making any attempt to attack the bowling, which, however, was certainly good.

Two more defeats followed: the Sussex Martlets won by 6 wickets and WM Bradley's XI, for whom CNG Eaton scored 137, won by 153 runs. This run of misfortune ended with the defeat of Hampton Wick in a match which finished in high drama:

> The last pair were together when the final over was called, and Jeffery, who was bowling, placed eight men within about five yards of the bat, but managed to hit the stumps with his fourth ball.

The Week ended with another visit to Ardingly where the Old Ardinians were successful once again.

Jeffery's bowling during the 1935 Week is worth setting out in full:

v The Stoics	17-4-41-4
v Leicester Ivanhoe	28-2-106-7
v Sussex Martlets	14-0-54-5
v WM Bradley's XI	10.3-0-46-2
v Hampton Wick	19.3-5-46-4
v Old Ardinians	15-5-41-5

His 27 wickets is still the highest number of wickets taken in the Week.

Despite being generally a poor summer the 1936 Week might have been worse:

> The O.Js. were fortunate in being able to get so much cricket into their week. Pitches, particularly before lunch, were always slow – sometimes very slow – but except on the Thursday, when rain only ceased for a few hours during the afternoon, they dried appreciably during the day. Hot sun on the Tuesday and Wednesday afternoons turned wickets into "glue-pots" and accounted for the heavy defeats by Leicester Ivanhoe and Sussex Martlets.

The Stoics lost by 35 runs, largely thanks to Jeffery who took five for 55 and who then top-scored with 84. Leicester Ivahoe administered a very heavy defeat – the OHJs going down by 244 runs. WS Hurd, another Leicestershire player, had a great match, scoring 120 and taking six for 26. Another first-class player – AW Pewtress, formerly of Lancashire, and then teaching at Brighton Grammar School, top-scored for the Sussex Martlets who then routed the Old Hurst Johnians for 93. Rain halted the match against WM Bradley's XI after 27 overs. There was no sixth match this year so the Hampton Wick game brought the Week to an end. The OHJs reached 233 thanks to an unbeaten 100 from Weller. Hampton Wick held out for a draw with one wicket left following a top score of 72 by AES Rippon – the sixth first-class cricketer to appear in the 1936 Week.

In 1937 the weather was much better and more players were available. The Stoics match was a 12-a-side affair. There was another big total from the Leicester Ivanhoe – 264 for 9 declared – who then dismissed the OHJs for 115. This was largely due to the bowling of the young Jim Sperry who was just starting his 187-match career with Leicestershire in which he took 490 first-class wickets before he retired in 1952. As we shall see, he reappeared in the 1953 Week. WM Bradley's XI made way for Romany who won by 61 runs. JHKdeW Denning made one of his very few Cricket Week appearances. It was fortunate that he did so, because Romany, who made 141, dismissed the OHJs for 80 which would have been considerably less had Denning and Lattimer not added 34 for the last wicket. Hampton Wick won by 7 wickets to end a Week that one feels was not as happy as it might have been.

In 1938 the reporter in the *Hurst Johnian* was more upbeat and described the Week as:

> undoubtedly, one of the most enjoyable we have had since "Weeks" started. The weather was fine, the wickets excellent, the games were played in sporting spirit; in short, everyone, visitors as well as Old Johnians, seemed to be having a thoroughly good time. A goodly number turned up, and the captain's chief difficulty was not, as in former years, "whom can I get to play to-day?" but "Whom can I leave out?" To Mr Scott again, our very best thanks for so ably ministering to our bodily needs and comforts.

> Three matches won, one lost, one drawn, sums up the results, and the batting throughout the week was

attractive to watch. We do want more bowling, though. Any offers for 1939?

In the match against the Stoics Jeffery took six for 52 and was instrumental in a 39 run OHJ victory. This year there was no visit from the Leicester Ivanhoe, but a team of cadets from RAF Cranwell appeared instead to record a 192 run victory, BP Young scoring an unbeaten 130 for them which turned out to be the last century taken off OHJ bowling until HJJ Malcolm made 133* for the Stoics in 1956. Thanks to Weller (56) and Carr (73) and six for 89 by JK Rhoden, the Sussex Martlets were beaten by 91 runs.

Further heavy scoring occurred in the Romany match. Leo Ricketts made 140 out of an OHJ total of 318 for 7 declared. In reply Romany were 225 for 7 with the borrowed Bill Coley making 57. This year Hampton Wick suffered a heavy defeat. The OHJs declared at 301 for 7 – Ricketts and Rhoden making 150 for the first wicket. Hampton Wick then collapsed for 93 with main damage being done by Lattimer with four for 33.

In contrast the 1939 Week was not one of the most memorable. The report says it all:

> From a weather point of view, this was the worst cricket week ever experienced. In two matches not a ball could be bowled, and though a start was made on Wednesday, rain stopped the game soon after lunch. Still those who came enjoyed the Week and squash and football matches against the Stoics on the Monday took the place of the cricket.

The matches against the Stoics and W Riches' XI (replacing Romany) were washed out and the Sussex Martlets game ended after the Martlets had reached 173 for 5. The two games which were completed were very close. RAF Cranwell batted first and made 136 with Jeffery taking eight for 37. The OHJs fell one run short. The last match was against Hampton Wick. It only lasted 56 overs but the match was a triumph for MA who made 43 out of an OHJ total of 122 and then had figures of 10-6-10-5 to dismiss Hampton Wick for 63.

That very same evening he announced his resignation as captain of the OJs so his performance on the field earlier in the day came as a fitting end to the excellent work he had done on the field for the Week. The nomination of a successor as captain was left to a later date. Twenty-two days later the Second World War began.

Interlude
1940 to 1946

No OHJ matches had been played against the College during the First World War although the fixture was revived very quickly in 1919. In 1940, however, the usual Bank Holiday match between the College and the OHJs was arranged for Monday 13 May, just three days after Churchill became Prime Minister and the German offensive in France and the Low Countries had started. The Government had also cancelled the Bank Holiday.

As a result, only five OHJs arrived for the match. Unsurprisingly one of them was, inevitably, MA who was accompanied by RW Coley, K Lock, DJ Church and JM Esdaile. As one might expect a new match was arranged, and what became known as MA Pitcher's XI took the field against the College. His team was made up of the five OHJs, two masters – H Coulthurst and RE Bury, and four of the Westminster School boys – SJN Nicol, KAH Hinge, JJ Bates and WF Moss – who had been evacuated to the College.

The College batted first and declared at 167-7 and MA Pitcher's XI finished on 112 for 6. Probably not very exciting but, in view of what was going on across the Channel, really rather English.

Chapter Four

MA Pitcher Part 2: 1947 to 1972

Although the war in Europe ended on 8 May 1945, no attempt was made to revive the OHJ Cricket Week for August. There was, however, an OHJ match against the College which was played on Saturday 7 July. The College had prospered during the war years and the cricket had maintained a good standard. The match was won by the College who, batting first, made 205 – Denis Jeffery five for 89 and JN Lock five for 69. The OHJs were bowled out for 103 after Charles Carr and Leo Ricketts had put on 39 for the first wicket. The damage was done by Stanley Simmons – later a power in OHJ cricket – who took five for 24 in 11 overs. The College team contained four players who were to play major roles in OHJ cricket – John Neal, Michael Watkins, Bob Schad and the aforementioned Stanley Simmons. The OHJ side consisted of Carr, Ricketts, Coley, JN Lock, Lintott, Jeffery, HP Lock, Rawkins, Stanley, Goodger and, last but by no means least, MA Pitcher.

In the March 1946 issue of the *Hurst Johnian* it was announced that there would be 1st and 2nd XI OHJ matches against the College and that the Week would take place between 5 and 9 August. This was mentioned again in the July issue, but nothing further happened. It has proved to be impossible to find out what went wrong, but presumably there were problems over finding enough players and arranging five fixtures.

However, the Week was successfully revived the following year and on Monday 4 August 1947 the 21st Old Hurst Johnian Cricket Week got under way with a match against W Riches' XII who were defeated by an innings and 111 runs. Laurie Henwood, in his first Cricket Week match, scored 53, his driving being described as 'masterly'. Also making their Cricket Week debuts were John Neal, Captain of Cricket in 1945 and who was to play one match for

Sussex in 1951, and Stanley Simmons, the 1946 Captain who was later to become Sir Stanley Simmons and President of the Royal College of Obstetricians and Gynaecologists. Other newcomers were RE Miller, David Pike whose cricket bag was always filled with caps and blazers from various wandering clubs, Bob Schad, who took six for 5 in the second W Riches' innings, and Michael Watkins. The mixture of young newcomers and old hands such as the elegant batsman Leo Ricketts, now Captain of the Week, Charles Carr, WH Weller, DM Wood and Denis Jeffery was very promising. For the first time MA did not feel the need to play.

Unusually for a summer such as 1947 the Leicester Ivanhoe match was rained off, but Wednesday dawned fair for the OHJs to defeat the Sussex Martlets by 19 runs, David Pike taking six for 40. However, the real highlight of the game, it seems, was the presence among the spectators of Jack Hobbs whose son Len was playing for the Martlets. The Stoics were defeated by 12 runs before the Week ended with the game against Hampton Wick on what was described as 'a bowler's wicket'. Laurie Henwood took eight for 40 as Hampton Wick were dismissed for 69. Leo Ricketts steered his side to victory with an unbeaten 47 out of 97.

MA must have been delighted. He played in one match – against the Stoics when the report stated that 'the redoubtable MA Pitcher... can still produce a snorter when it is badly wanted.' Nineteen players had been available. Of the eight new players, five were destined to play a considerable and lengthy part in OHJ cricket.

In 1948 a Saturday match was added. The opponents for many years were the Repton Pilgrims who were on their Southern Tour and who had played the College 1st XI as long ago as 1920. The fixture lasted until 1968 since when the Buccaneers have been the Saturday opponents. On the Monday rain washed out a match against Horley – a fixture that was never revived. There was no play before lunch in the Leicester Ivanhoe match. When play did start, David Pike fell flat on his face when delivering the first ball. He recovered to take six for 24 helping the OHJs to a comfortable win. The Sussex Martlets were also defeated thanks to Peter English who took six for 4 in his first OHJ game. A very effective bowler, it was a pity that his service with the Hong Kong Police prevented him from appearing more often. The Stoics needed 178 to win but, despite the presence of SC Gobey who had played a few matches for Warwickshire in 1947, collapsed for 41 with the wickets being shared by Pike, Henwood and English. The rain returned on the Friday with a downpour ending the Hampton Wick match after 5.4 overs. Hampton Wick were then defeated at squash.

The weather improved enough to start the Repton Pilgrims game at midday on a 'a drying difficult pitch'. The OHJs reached 152 thanks to an unbeaten 53 from wicketkeeper John Neal who conceded only one bye all week. WAS Wesson performed the hat trick when he dismissed Davis, Schad and Gerrard. Rain, 45 minutes before the close of play, saved the Pilgrims who had reached 38 for 8.

It was a good Week with the side being thought to be stronger than in 1947 which, at the time, had been thought to be the strongest ever. No match had been lost in either season and there had obviously been a number of good individual performances. The debut of MA's son George should be noted: he too was destined to play a considerable part in OHJ cricket.

From all accounts 1949 was another good Week. The Eton Ramblers, making their first appearance in the Week, were defeated by 24 runs thanks to six for 49 from Stan Simmons. Some rain made the wicket easier for the next match in which Leicester Ivanhoe suffered a very heavy defeat, losing by 202 runs. Jack Youngman, reappearing for the first time since 1935, showed that he had lost none of his skill by scoring an unbeaten 175. After this onslaught Leicester Ivanhoe collapsed for 61 with Denis Jeffery taking five for 25 and Tokio Hill, in one of his rare appearances, four for 16.

The next match was against the Sussex Martlets whose

team contained the future South African Test player Paul Winslow who, at this time, was considering qualifying for Sussex. He made only 1 in a Martlet total of 205 (Laurie Henwood five for 52), but still left his mark on the match. The OHJ batting was not very successful and with 15 minutes left the total was 130 for 7. Eight minutes later Bob Schad was lbw to Winslow who then dismissed Rawkins. With three balls remaining, 'Peter Christie... lacking in elegance played out the over.' Winslow finished with three for 22.

Against the Stoics the OHJs declared at 234 for 9. The Stoics saved the game having reached 181 for 9. We are told that MA 'sent down five great overs to take four for 10' and that in the final over Denis Jeffery 'missed the stumps by the odd coat of varnish with his last ball.' The Hampton Wick match was drawn. Jack Youngman made 140 out of 198, having hit 2 sixes and 21 fours. The match ended in a draw with Hampton Wick who needed 245, being 30 runs short with one wicket left.

The Repton Pilgrims arrived on Saturday and inflicted the first defeat since 1939. It was a powerful Pilgrim side containing four first-class cricketers – GL Willatt of Cambridge University, Nottinghamshire and Derbyshire, PA Kelland of Cambridge University and Sussex, JRR Holmes of Sussex and last, but by no means least, BH Valentine of Oxford University, Kent and England. In a relatively low-scoring game the Repton Pilgrims won by 4 wickets. Willatt made 19, Holmes 19*, Kelland 38*. Valentine made 5 before being 'well-bowled by Henwood' who had also dismissed Willatt.

Jack Youngman scored 395 runs during the Week and averaged 79.00. This beat the record of Charles Carr who had scored 327 as long ago as 1928.

The Duck Club was founded in 1950 with the first six members joining during the course of the Week. Charles Carr was the first to fail to score and so he naturally became the President. He was soon followed by Leo Ricketts, Bill Coley, George Pitcher, Bob Schad and, of all players, Jack Youngman.

By 1956 a list of duck types had been compiled. The categories are as follows:

1. Duckling – ordinary simple duck
2. Adolescent – first ball duck
3. Premature – adolescent before duckling duck
4. Adult – both duckling duck and adolescent duck
5. Broody – duck incubating over 30 minutes
6. Caesarean – first ball of innings duck
7. Brood – two or more of any duck type in succession
8. Stillborn – run out without receiving a ball
9. Prodigy – carrying bat throughout innings for not out duck
10. Illegitimate – playing for opposition duck
11. Impotent Drake – no further interest in ducks

Non-qualifying types:
12. Gleam in the drake's eye – 0 not out
13. Anxious look in the drake's eye – retired hurt

The constitution is very clear about the conduct of affairs. The badge of membership is 'a tie of a dark blue background surmounted at regular intervals by a Crest of a nought-balancing, Pavilion-walking Duck, facing west'. This tie has to be worn on the first and last days of the Week and at the annual Dinner. It is also stipulated that on no account may ties 'be used for any purpose whatever other than that for which their sartorial shape is intended.'

It is a requirement that the first run of all non-members should be applauded suitably. A further clause states that: 'The first occasion of qualification on the part of any non-member shall be applauded enthusiastically, although membership is a matter to be deplored.' On his return to the pavilion the new member is presented with his tie and the pavilion bell is rung. It is, of course, very important that candidates should be fully aware of the situation as there have, over the years, been one or two embarrassing occasions. There has also, of course, been much hilarity and jollification. Unsurprisingly the motto is Omnibus Dux.

The batting was not so successful in 1950 although the weather was good, and it was felt that the wickets were the best since the War. This year there was a break with tradition and the Bank Holiday Monday match against Cuckfield was played there. There has always been a strong link between the College and Cuckfield and at the time of writing three or four members of the Cuckfield 1st XI are OHJs. There were also a number of matches between the Common Room and Cuckfield in the 1970s. In 1950 IB Ingall and F Mitchell, both OHJs, played for Cuckfield. The OHJs lost a low-scoring match: Laurie Henwood took five for 41 to help dismiss Cuckfield for 129. The OHJs were 102 for 9 at tea, needing a further 28 runs, but the last wicket pair of MA and David Pike could only manage 14 of them. Returning to the College for the next match, Leicester Ivanhoe were clearly the stronger side winning by 75 runs.

After a delayed start the Sussex Martlets, strengthened by the presence of the Cambridge Blue David Dickinson, won by two wickets off the second ball of the last over. There was a comfortable win against the Stoics. The OHJs declared at 250 for 4 after Leo Ricketts had made 54 and Laurie Henwood had scored 81. Tight bowling took the OHJs to a 124-run victory. Another powerful Repton Pilgrims side won by six wickets. It was noted that 'Valentine played every shot with confident ease', at least until he was caught by Bob Schad off David Pike for 19.

The Week of 1951 was one of the wettest on record. Not once was there a full day's play and three matches were cancelled. This year the Eton Ramblers became permanent visitors to the Week, but we are told that the 'only cricket played was in the home changing room with a stump and a ping pong ball.' After a 2.15 pm start the Leicester Ivanhoe won by 37 runs. The Sussex Martlets game never started and was abandoned after lunch. 'Henwood and GM Pitcher took on Martlets opponents and beat them at squash.'

The Stoics game came to an end in mid-afternoon. The *Hurst Johnian* reports that after 'ten minutes of torrential rain the wicket was flooded, puddles formed in the outfield and the match was abandoned.' Victory over Hampton Wick followed after a delayed start with Carter taking five for 19 in thirteen overs to produce a 56 runs victory. There was no play against the Repton Pilgrims and the 1951 Cricket Week report concludes that 'as we left, the roads were almost under water and the Downs were blotted out by sheets of driving rain.'

In the five Weeks since the War there had been 18 new players, but, of these, five belonged to the pre-war vintage so the pool of younger players was still on the low side. Most of those who came played in every match. This continued to be the pattern for many years. Nevertheless, the fixture list was developing: the scratch elevens had almost completely disappeared and the 1950s would see a set of regular opponents – Eton Ramblers, Leicester Ivanhoe, Sussex Martlets, the Stoics, Hampton Wick (who hosted a match on the Sunday before the Week began on the Bank Holiday Monday) and Repton Pilgrims. It was an enviable fixture list and, as we have seen, attracted a number of first-class cricketers.

1952 was described as one of the most enjoyable Weeks since the War although it was felt that the results were not as good as they should have been, possibly due to the 'strain of continuous play'. Again, the problem was lack of numbers. There was, however, one newcomer who was to become a very major contributor to OHJ cricket: his name was Keith Jenkin. Including the Sunday match against Hampton Wick seventeen players were used. Four players played in all six matches and another four in five. Of the 17 players nine had been at Hurst before the War so were the wrong side of 30. Not for the only time was the first part of the Week going to be far more successful than the last. The batting was stronger than ever before with a rate of 100 runs per hour being reached more than once. The bowling disappointed, but in two spells 'MA Pitcher twice alarmed the opposition by taking a quick wicket' and George Pitcher's fielding was described as being 'noticeable in every part of the field'.

Excelling with the off-drive and, at one point, scoring 64 in 43 minutes, Jack Youngman began the Week with 150 off the Eton Ramblers who were defeated by 173 runs. The match against Leicester Ivanhoe was drawn. Youngman with 56, followed by Leo Ricketts and Bob Schad in a partnership of 112 led to a declaration at 288 for 8. Despite the presence of the veteran Leslie Berry, who had retired from first-class cricket the summer before and was now coaching at Uppingham, Leicester Ivanhoe struggled to 132 for 9 with Carter taking five for 32.

A Laurie Henwood century, strangely his only Cricket Week hundred, and another partnership – this time of 100 by Leo Ricketts and Bob Schad – enabled the OHJs to declare and set the Sussex Martlets 293 to win. After his long innings Henwood then bowled 28 overs to take five for 120 taking his side to a 58-run victory. Defeat by the Stoics followed the next day and then on the Friday Hampton Wick won for the first time in 11 matches since the War. This was:

> due to some indifferent OJ batting following some unenterprising tactics by our visitors who batted four hours to make 180 runs and left us half that time in which to get the runs which led to over-anxiety to force the pace which led to some faulty strokes, bad running between the wickets, and our subsequent narrow failure by 6 runs. No one showed the necessary determination and concentration which could have won this match with ease.

Tiredness would seem to have taken its toll and perhaps there was less disappointment than there might otherwise have been when the Repton Pilgrims match was rained off.

Cheerfulness, however, has always been a keynote of OHJ cricket and we find the 1953 Week described as 'blessed with ideal weather, a complete success.' Seventeen players were available including E Hindsley from West Africa and Peter Christie from the Sudan, but 'other faces were not so plentiful'.

Facing a target of 160 against the Eton Ramblers for whom GHGM 'Buns' Cartwright, who might well have been called the MA Pitcher of Eton Rambler cricket and who was a pre-First World War Oxford blue, had opened the batting, the OHJs reached 85 for 1 but were unable to press home their advantage and finished up losing by 28 runs. Leicester Ivanhoe were too strong. This time Leslie Berry was accompanied by his former county colleague Jim Sperry who, it will be remembered, had appeared in the 1937 match. Only Berry who made 47 out of a total of 196 for 7 played Keith Jenkin's 'flighted off-spinners with any confidence', Jenkin taking five for 52. Sperry then bowled the Ivanhoe to victory with six for 44 in 18 overs. His two visits to Hurst had netted him eleven wickets for 93 runs.

The Sussex Martlets were defeated by 100 runs. After the OHJs had declared at 191 for 6 – Jenkin 58 and Neal 60 having added 108 for the 4th wicket – the Martlets were dismissed for 91, Jenkin taking six for 40 and Carter four for 18. Keith Jenkin was to the fore again against the Stoics, 'thumping the ball vigorously to all parts of the field' in making 95. The Stoics needed 225, but after Peter Christie had taken the first wicket, Laurie Henwood, wicketless thus far in the Week, took nine for 52, bowling unchanged for 14.3 overs.

In what was described as 'a lethargic performance' in heavy and oppressive weather Hampton Wick were victorious for the second year running, this time by 136 runs. For once the Repton Pilgrims game was unaffected by bad weather and was described as 'a wonderful match and a perfect climax to an extremely successful Week'. The Repton Pilgrims were dismissed for 191. Carter (47) and Henwood (94) added 148 for the second wicket to help the OHJs to a 5-wicket win.

As far as first-class cricket is concerned the summer of 1954 was the worst since 1888 and eventually turned out to be the wettest cricket season of the 20th century. It was not the worst Cricket Week, but it certainly ranks with 1939, 1951 and 1985 as one of the wettest.

The Eton Ramblers innings of 229 for 7 declared lasted for 83 overs with the debutant George Hill bowling 26 overs to take two for 53. Laurie Henwood made 97 but it was not enough, the Ramblers winning by 27 runs. There was then a comfortable 155 run victory over Leicester Ivanhoe. A second wicket stand of 152 by Keith Jenkin (107) and Laurie Henwood (61) led to a declaration at 286 for 7. A good all-round bowling performance dismissed the Ivanhoe for 131. Despite five for 55 from Hill and Jenkin's four for 21, the Sussex Martlets won by 26 runs. The Stoics won a 12-a-side match by 51 runs, despite six for 42 by Frank Allen and 58 from Henwood.

The last two matches – against Hampton Wick and Repton Pilgrims – were rained off. In view of the future of the Week the most significant event, however, was the arrival of George Hill who was destined to succeed MA as Manager in 1973. The report has this to say:

> ... Hill playing in his first Week, and something of an unknown quantity. It is to his credit that he played consistently well and untiringly, his clever variation of pace frequently beating the bat.

We are also given a list of those present which gives a feel of how things were 66 years ago:

> Leo Ricketts with his dog and Mannikins
> Charles Carr, President of the Duck Club who lived up to the Club's traditions against the Stoics
> John Rawkins with the inevitable golf clubs and birthday cards
> Bill Coley with his early morning tea
> "Colonel" Kup with his electric kettle which was definitely working by the final morning
> Dennis Jeffery
> Jack Youngman with his weather reports
> Derek Wood the tea planter from Assam
> Laurie Henwood without his fiancée
> George Pitcher with his pint of Jersey milk and John Molyneaux, "the new boy".
> From various parts of Sussex came John Neal, Keith Jenkin, Michael Watkins, George Hill and Frank Allen all of whom were delighted to welcome the Headmaster,

PW (Scott) and BIP (Pocock).

In 1955 the Week began on the Sunday, the Headmaster, Canon Howard, having given permission for cricket on a Sunday – provided that the game started after midday. Thus, the visits to Hampton Wick finished and Romany reappeared until their withdrawal in 2018. Laurie Henwood, now captain, took six for 27 to bowl his side to victory. There was a comfortable win against the Eton Ramblers watched by 'a large gathering of spectators scattered beneath the chestnuts on the bank.' Jack Youngman and Keith Jenkin shared an opening partnership of 129 against Leicester Ivanhoe with Youngman going on to an unbeaten 140. Despite the presence of the Leicestershire opening bowler, Brian Boshier who took one for 50 in 13 overs, the Ivanhoe lost by 120 runs.

The Sussex Martlets, containing three members of the College staff – Reg Ruddock, Harry Maxwell and Michael Bickmore – were beaten by four wickets with a few minutes to spare. Even closer, however, was the match against the Stoics which was also notable for its fast scoring. Keith Jenkin – 74 and Jack Youngman – 75 – made 138 for the first wicket. George Pitcher then made 50 which led to a declaration at 269 for 7. Needing 270 the Stoics, thanks to an opening partnership of 105 by Gerald Plumbly and the Middlesex player, HJJ Malcolm, reached 215 for 3 at which point three further wickets fell. Then followed a ten-minute onslaught by PA Johnson which lifted the score to 261 for eight. Needing four off the last over – bowled by Bob Schad – Iberson was bowled with the first ball, two more runs were scored before Deigan lofted the fifth ball gently to Stan Simmons at mid-off and the OHJs had won by one run.

For some long-forgotten reason the Hampton Wick fixture was replaced by one with Sussex Young Amateurs. Described as 'much enjoyed' it ended with a Young Amateurs victory. Three of the previous four Repton Pilgrims games had been rained off. 1955 was different and, although the Pilgrims were accused of delaying their declaration until they had reached 223 for 9 with Hill taking seven for 78 in 26 overs, they made light work of the OHJ batting which succumbed in 80 minutes for a total of 51. PA Kelland, the Oxford blue and occasional Sussex player, took six for 23.

1956 was yet another summer that was typical of the 1950s – cool, windy and frequently very wet. The Week, however, did not suffer as badly as might have been expected. Romany were eventually defeated by three wickets. Needing only 136 for victory RRA Knight and George Hill made 87 for the first wicket. The score was taken on to 127 for 4 but three wickets then fell rapidly and the OHJs, guided by George Pitcher, struggled to 139 for 7. On the Bank Holiday Monday the Eton Ramblers game lasted for 10 overs before rain caused an abandonment. In a low-scoring match Leicester Ivanhoe were beaten by 50 runs. Batting first the OHJs reached 129 – John Neal having scored 47 and only two other players – Laurie Henwood and Leo Ricketts – getting into double figures. Spooner bowled unchanged for 27.1 overs to take six for 65: it would not happen today. Leicester Ivanhoe were dismissed by George Hill (five for 13) and Bob Schad (four for 31) for 79. The Sussex Martlets were beaten in another low scoring match the day before the Stoics were victorious by 152 runs. HJJ Malcolm made an unbeaten 133 which enabled the Stoics to set the OHJs a target of 230 who could only reach 79 with J Iberson taking five for 17 in 5.4 overs.

Rain returned on the Friday and only 11 overs were possible in the match against the Sussex Young Amateurs whose opening batsmen were the Oxford Blue RHC Waters and Richard Langridge who was about to follow his father James and his uncle John into the Sussex team. There was play on the Saturday, but it was all over in 63.5 overs. On a wet wicket, the Repton Pilgrims, aided by two first-class players in PA Kelland, whose presence has been noted before, and JF Mendl of Scotland and MCC fame, dismissed the OHJs for 84 before knocking off the runs for the loss of only three wickets.

The weather was better in 1957, at least until the Friday when the Sussex Young Amateurs match was washed out. On the following day a start was made to the Repton Pilgrims game only for it to brought to a premature end as the Repton Pilgrims were starting on their target of 177.

The Week began well with a 34-run victory over Romany. Michael Bickmore, son of AF Bickmore of Kent, and a member of the College staff who had the distinction of having been Colin Cowdrey's captain at Tonbridge, made 117 while Gerald Plumbly was busy taking five for 44. The next day another Jack Youngman century – 128 – dominated the Eton Ramblers game. This time Youngman was sixth out with the score at 223. Needing 245 the Ramblers had no answer to the bowling of Michael Watkins who took six for 29 to help dismiss them for 110.

131 from John Neal led to an OHJ total of 240 for 5 declared and on to a 120-run victory over Leicester Ivanhoe who, this year, had no first-class players in their ranks. The Sussex Martlets, aided by Reg Ruddock, who scored 50, and Harry Maxwell, won by 86 runs. Apart from Laurie Henwood, 60*, no one had any answer to the bowling of Bill Stewart who took five for 37. This game is, of course, far more notable for the fact that it was the last time that MA took the field in a Cricket Week match. He batted at Number 11 and made 4 in a last wicket partnership of 12 with JMA Ellis.

The Stoics game was lost by five wickets. Iberson, who posed a number of problems for the OHJs over the years, took eight for 44 as the OHJs struggled to 133. In reply HJJ Malcolm (52*) and MH Bushby (57), a Cambridge Blue and captain in 1954, made 87 for the first wicket, helping the Stoics to a five-wicket win.

1958 was yet another poor summer. The weather was at its worst. Two matches – Leicester Ivanhoe and the Stoics when Marsh took six for 27 – were abandoned half – way through and the Sussex Young Amateurs game never started. Except for the Eton Ramblers game, all matches were 'played in gloomy conditions with greyness overhead and dampness underfoot'. Nevertheless 27 players – including three from the 1958 College 1st XI – were available.

The Romany match ended in a draw with the OHJs 67 runs behind with one wicket remaining and Laurie Henwood having scored 73 out of 93 added while he was at the wicket. The Eton Ramblers were beaten by an innings and 98 runs. They were dismissed for 38, Jenkin taking four for 1. The OHJs gained a lead of 161, George Hill top-scoring with an unbeaten 38. Batting a second time the Ramblers lost their first wicket at 0. Four byes then ensued before the second, third and fourth wickets fell with no further addition to the score which was then taken to 41 before another collapse took place – 41 for 4 very soon becoming 49 for 9. The last wicket added 14. George Hill had figures of 5-3-4-3 and Michael Watkins 3-2-2-1.

The Sussex Martlets match produced another batting collapse. The OHJs batted first. Jack Youngman left at 43. Keith Jenkin and John Neal then added 120 for the second wicket before Neal was lbw for 64. Jenkin – 75 – followed at 171. Stewart then proceeded to run through the rest of the OHJ batting taking five wickets in 12 balls including the hat trick – George Pitcher, David Pike and Michael Watkins – to give him final figures of eight for 46. Five OHJ batsmen, including Duck Club President Charles Carr, failed to score. The Martlets made slow progress and reached 157 for 6 in 55 overs. The Repton Pilgrims were victorious by five wickets. On a wet wicket the OHJs were bowled out for 45 – Jack Youngman making 20 out of the 27 scored while he was at the wicket. It took the Repton Pilgrims 24.1 overs to make the 46 required for victory.

1959 was the best summer of the decade. For once there were no abandonments, no cancellations and all seven matches ran their full course. Romany were beaten by five wickets in a low-scoring game in which Keith Jenkin took five for 27. In the next match an unbeaten 117 by John Neal enabled the OHJs to declare at 236 for 4. The Eton Ramblers reached 215 for 9, George Hill having taken four for 36. There was a comfortable win over Leicester Ivanhoe with John Neal again to the fore with an innings of 86.

The Sussex Martlets won a low-scoring match by 7 wickets. The Stoics, however, were beaten by 99 runs. Needing 210, they collapsed for 110 with Harry Maxwell taking six for 33. The last two matches were lost – the Sussex Young Amateurs won by six wickets and the Repton Pilgrims won by 70 runs. The latter game was Bill Coley's last. Always a great supporter of the Week in every way, he will always be remembered for his lament when dismissed – 'Why am I always out to the best ball of the day?'

Around this time MA suggested that he might retire, but the idea was laughed out of existence. However, a very significant development for the future did take place – George Hill became Assistant Manager. MA had recognised the value of an OHJ member of the College staff.

Generally speaking, 1960 was another gloomy summer, but the Cricket Week was an exception: the report in the *Hurst Johnian* stating that MA 'even managed to organize the weather which was fine and sunny except for Tuesday'. Although it was felt that there was still a shortage of bowlers a number of younger OHJs – Berks, Waterfall, the Carr twins, BBG Jeffery and, most significantly, Chris Hodgkins, an excellent fielder, made their first appearances.

For Romany D Russell took seven for 65 as the OHJS struggled to 116 in 46.3 overs. Romany took almost as long – 46.1 overs – to get the runs for the loss of five wickets. Further low scoring followed the next day with the Eton Ramblers dismissing the OHJs for 88 to win by 67 runs.

Rain ruined the Leicester Ivanhoe match. With two first-class cricketers – the Leicestershire pair of RA Diment and JM Josephs – the Ivanhoe had reached 106 for 4 when the rain came. The Sussex Martlets game ended in a draw with the OHJs 38 runs short of their target of 207.

The Stoics were beaten by five wickets with three minutes to spare. The OHJs reached their target in 44.4 overs, finding run-scoring easier than their opponents who had used up 75.4 overs to reach 169. Against the Sussex Young Amateurs, Jenkin made 128 before lunch and the OHJs were able to declare at 242 for 7, but consistent batting by the Amateurs enabled them to win by 1 wicket with two balls remaining – the winning hit being a six over the head of the shortest OHJ fielder. Regrettably his name has not been recorded for posterity.

The Week ended with what looks like a rather uninteresting draw against the Repton Pilgrims despite an unbeaten 81 from Laurie Henwood. The report of the Week concludes with thanks to MA 'for his fine organization and unbounding enthusiasm which gives so much pleasure to so many'.

The 1961 Week is 'remembered for the most consistent and entertaining batting since the War', but what was more significant, especially in view of the reservations about the bowling which had been expressed the year before, was the arrival of Willie Welch whose career as opening bowler and more than useful lower order batsman was to last until 1996.

The Romany match was drawn. The Eton Ramblers, boosted by the presence of RVC Robins who made several appearances for Middlesex, achieved a two wicket win in a 12-a-side match. Leicester Ivanhoe, strengthened yet again by the presence of two first-class cricketers in Josephs and EF Phillips, were unable to secure the last OHJ wicket to force a win.

The Sussex Martlets declared at 219 for 8, Keith Jenkin having taken five for 58. He then scored 47 before Chris Hodgkins, 105, and Laurie Henwood, 57*, took the OHJs to an eight-wicket victory. Further good batting – this time from Bob Schad, 114*, and Denis Bradley, 52*, left the Stoics needing 238 to win. They fell short by 108 runs – Denis Jeffery finishing with four for 3. There was a delayed start against the Sussex Young Amateurs who eventually won by 53 runs thanks to an unbeaten 86 from PRV Ledden (who later made 35 appearances for Sussex) and seven for 55 from J Trevett.

The final match against the Repton Pilgrims was won by 75 runs. Keith Jenkin, 70, and Laurie Henwood, 54, enabled the OHJs to make 166 despite five batsmen failing to score – Hodgkins, Schad, Welch, Hill and Watkins. They were almost joined by John Neal. We are told:

> So, to the final match which opened in sensational fashion with Jenkin apparently determined to enlist Neal into the Duck Club. A more likely explanation for an impossible call for a run from the first ball is that he was anxious to end a succession of failures against Repton. Fortunately, the wicketkeeper failed to gather an accurate return cleanly and Jenkin and Neal went on to score 43 invaluable runs against the most hostile bowling of the Week.

John Neal, whose last match was in 1965, never did join the Duck Club.

The 'hostile bowling' was produced by Kelland and Fletcher, the latter taking five for 39 and at one stage taking five wickets for four runs in 12 balls.

MA had now been manager for 41 years. Again, the report was full of praise for him. He 'continues to manage and organize the Week with such success and such infectious enthusiasm.'

Despite a lack of sunshine with rain on Monday and a delayed start on Tuesday, 1962 was another successful Week. There was again a good blend of youth and experience. Romany were beaten by 7 wickets, but the Eton Ramblers match only lasted seven overs before rain forced an abandonment. This, in turn, led to a delayed start against Leicester Ivanhoe who won by four wickets after the OHJs had declared at 214 for 7 with Chris Hodgkins making 77.

A good all-round performance produced a 55-run victory over the Sussex Martlets. This was followed by a two-wicket win against the Stoics. For once the Sussex Young Amateurs were defeated. The Repton Pilgrims match ended in a draw. Chris Hodgkins was praised for his 'aggressive and consistent batting'. He had scored 2, 8*, 77, 50, 82, 72 and 65* averaging 71.00. These were very good figures for a batman on the Hurst wicket of those days.

The 1963 Week, for which MA was thanked for 'always doing something to make the Week more enjoyable not only for us but also for our guests and opponents', was noteworthy in two ways: seven full days' play and the debut of Dick Smart who was destined to become Cricket Week's leading wicket taker. He began by bowling 21 overs in Romany's innings and taking three for 70, but it was not enough to prevent Romany from winning by two wickets.

The Eton Ramblers, whose innings was opened by CTM Pugh who had captained Gloucestershire in the two preceding seasons, declared at 222 for nine which had taken them 61 overs. The OHJs reached 219 for 9 in just 39 overs. Leicester Ivanhoe - Smart six for 46 - were beaten by 35 runs. Chris Hodgkins, with 84*, was the only batsman on either side to make a decent score. Batting was obviously more straightforward on the following day against the Sussex Martlets when the OHJs were able to declare at 265 for 5, Hodgkins again to the fore with 122*. Keith Jenkin then took seven for 78 but the Martlets held out and were 33 runs behind with one wicket left. The Stoics had a comfortable win, only Jenkin with 63 making any impression. The Sussex Young Amateurs were defeated by 61 runs, a good all-round performance. Bryan Valentine was due to bat at No. 6 for the Repton Pilgrims but, as they won by six wickets, the services of the former Kent and England player were not required. It was also Jack Youngman's last match - he scored 17 and bowled the last over.

The 38th Week which, 'surely must be recorded as the most successful and enjoyable ever', was lengthened to eight matches, running from Saturday to Saturday. It was still very much a bachelor week and most of the players were accommodated in one of the dormitories. Robin Carr remembers that when he was the most junior player it was his job to make and serve early morning tea in company with the most senior player - MA himself. Meals were provided in the Tuck Shop but did not include an evening meal. Several pubs were visited each evening before ending up at the New Inn in Hurstpierpoint which was always the prelude to a motor car race back to the College either via Western Road or College Lane. On one occasion a group of hungry players, led by a very eminent surgeon, had the temerity to break into the Tuck Shop and help themselves to quantities of eggs, bacon, tomatoes, sausages and bread for a late evening meal. Unfortunately, they had eaten the supplies for the next day's breakfast.

The new opponents were the Free Foresters whose side contained two first-class cricketers in John Bartlett, an Oxford Blue who also played for Sussex, and the Cambridge Blue David Dickinson. In addition, the batting was opened by the eminent journalist and Test Match Special commentator, Christopher Martin-Jenkins whose son Robin was later on the College staff. Thanks to Dickinson, 50*, the Free Foresters were able to declare at 186 for 9. The OHJs won by three wickets with three balls of the last over remaining. Bartlett – five for 81 – and Dickinson bowled all but ten of the 53.3 overs.

There was a comfortable victory over Romany with Willie Welch taking four for 14 in ten overs. The Eton Ramblers won by 52 runs. Only Keith Jenkin with 51 got past 20 in the OHJ innings as JCB Russell took six for 60. This was followed by a 44-run victory over Leicester Ivanhoe and a 107-run win against the Sussex Martlets. Jenkin, 84, and Hodgkins, 100*, led to an OHJ declaration at 250 for 4. Jenkin then took five for 32 to help dismiss the Martlets for 143. An innings of 116 by J Hyams helped the Stoics to set a target of 235. A third wicket stand of 160 by Hodgkins, 82, and George Pitcher, 65, took the OHJs to a six-wicket victory. Keith Jenkin had a field day against the Sussex Young Cricketers when his eight for 19 brought about a 35 run OHJ victory. Yet again the Repton Pilgrims match was ruined by rain – only 53 overs were bowled.

1965 was rather an ordinary summer, although MA was now something of an institution. In the words of the *Hurst Johnian*:

He has firmly established a Cricket Week which for hospitality coupled with good and enjoyable cricket against a most interesting variety of opponents can scarcely be equalled.

It was Bob Schad's first year as captain and Keith Jenkin passed 2000 runs – at this stage only Jack Youngman and Laurie Henwood had scored more. The Duck Club was in its fifteenth year and there were now 40 OHJs whose membership was to be deplored.

The Free Foresters won a low-scoring match by three runs. Needing 130 to win, Keith Jenkin and Guy Williams made 49 for the first wicket. Four more wickets fell for six runs before BBG Jeffery helped Jenkin get the score to 103. Jenkin was eventually dismissed for 83 which made it 116 for 8. The ninth wicket fell at 125 and one run later Smart was bowled. Derek Henderson, a former Oxford Blue, took five for 34 and John Bartlett was amongst the wickets again with five for 46. The next day Romany struggled to 126 in 48 overs – Willie Welch five for 48. The OHJs proceeded to win comfortably by eight wickets – Keith Jenkin 81*.

This was followed by 1.25 inches of rain which meant the cancellation of the Eton Ramblers match and a post-lunch start against Leicester Ivanhoe. For the OHJs Bob Finch, a member of staff and a former Berkshire player, made 71 out of a total of 185. Leicester Ivanhoe fell short by 14 runs with four wickets in hand.

Making his first Cricket Week appearance since 1947, Max Rhoden took two for 32 against the Sussex Martlets who were beaten by 61 runs. Earlier the OHJs had declared at 205 for 2 – Guy Williams 93* and Rick Holgate 87*. Bowling unchanged, Dick Smart demolished the Stoics batting in taking seven for 32 in 16.2 overs to engineer a 135-run victory. Smart was to the fore on the following day; this time he took seven for 85 in 29.2 overs as the OHJs defeated the Sussex Young Cricketers by 63 runs.

Alas the winning streak could not be maintained. Dick Smart was wicketless the next day as the Repton Pilgrims won by five wickets off the last ball of the match, having reached their target of 201 in 44 overs, compared with the snail-like performance of the OHJs who had needed 72 overs to reach 200.

Despite the 1966 weather being wet and cold, five full days' play was possible on the soft and slow wickets. David Dickinson and John Bartlett appeared again for the Free Foresters but the player to make the greatest impression was the young Tony Greig who was qualifying for Sussex. He opened the bowling taking four for 27 in 8.1 overs, to dismiss Jenkin, Hill, Smart and R Carswell. The Free Foresters needed 135 to win. The match ended with some spectacular hitting by Greig who finished off the match with a six off Jenkin over Malthouse Lane with the ball finally coming to rest in the far reaches of the East Field, at which point Greig pulled off his gloves, tucked his bat under his arm, said, 'Thank you, gentlemen' and made for the pavilion.

Although Dick Smart took five for 46 the Romany total of 182 for 8 declared was too much for the OHJs who, having been 80 for 9, were eventually dismissed for 112 after Smart and Bishop had added 32 for the tenth wicket. Rain brought an early end to the Eton Ramblers match. This was followed by an eight wicket win over Leicester Ivanhoe. The eminent South African cricket historian, Brian Bassano, was in the Sussex Martlets team which was unable to get anywhere near the target of 217. Bassano top-scored with 40 after Hodgkins, 94, narrowly missed his fourth century in five innings against the Sussex Martlets.

The Stoics match was curtailed by rain after 29 overs, but the weather improved on Friday for an OHJ 45 run victory over the Sussex Young Cricketers. Keith Jenkin took six for 42, bowling without a rest for 16.2 overs. The rain returned and for the fourth time not a ball could be bowled in the Repton Pilgrims match.

The 1967 Week was much better with eight full days of cricket apart from a short interruption in the Romany match. Laurie Henwood reappeared while Paul Ruddlesdin and Roger Goodacre made their first of many appearances.

There was a comment that the bowling lacked penetration, although it was noted that Dick Smart had taken twelve wickets in three matches before he left to get married.

The Free Foresters made 265 for 7 declared with MJL Willard, a former Cambridge Blue, making 161* and Smart taking five for 64. Consistent OHJ batting led to victory by one wicket. Romany were beaten by three wickets and the Eton Ramblers lost by 81 runs. The Leicester Ivanhoe match might have been described as slow-moving. It took 70 overs for the OHJs to reach 181 for 9 declared. Leicester Ivanhoe finished up 36 adrift with two wickets left.

With only one wicket left the Sussex Martlets were eleven runs away from victory. It was perhaps more noteworthy that 16 out of 22 batsmen were dismissed in single figures. The Stoics were bowled to victory by John Nagenda who later played for East Africa in the 1975 World Cup. The OHJs needed 150 to win, but they were all out for 88. Nagenda bowled unchanged and took eight for 36 in 18.1 overs.

The next day was even worse. The Sussex Young Cricketers, whose team contained four who were later to play first-class cricket – John Spencer, Alan Mansell, RNP Smyth and MT Barford, dismissed the OHJs for 76 and went on to win by eight wickets. Spencer took five for 21. The next day the Repton Pilgrims won a well-fought game by 28 runs.

1968 was described as a gloomy week, but it was reported that MA had 'continued to manage the Week with enthusiasm'. The Week was not without significance. The Repton Pilgrims, who had given up their Southern Tour, were replaced by the Buccaneers. Leicester Ivanhoe appeared for the last time and the Old Amplefordians replaced the Sussex Young Cricketers. The Sussex Martlets match was moved to Friday with the Old Amplefordians becoming the Wednesday opponents.

Dick Smart took six for 27 to help dismiss the Free Foresters for 67. He and Willie Welch – three for 37- bowled unchanged for 32.2 overs. It then took the OHJs 36 overs to reach 71-5. The next day, against Romany, Keith Jenkin made 90 out of 162 for 9 declared before Willie Welch took six for 52 to take the OHJs to a 30-run victory. Making 61 for Romany was Nick Searls who had just completed the first of his 37 years on the College staff. Jenkin took five for 25 to help dismiss the Eton Ramblers for 111. An eight wicket OHJ victory followed.

The last Leicester Ivanhoe match ended in a draw which, 51 years later, looks as though it was a rather boring affair. The Old Amplefordian match was rained off, but conditions improved on the following day when the Stoics were defeated by four wickets, Nagenda having taken four for 65. This match had to be played on the gym end of the square which meant a very long walk to and from the pavilion – even longer if you were out first ball as was Nagenda – bowled by Smart. The Sussex Martlets lost by 68 runs being dismissed for 99. The first Buccaneers match, which was Laurie Henwood's last, was drawn. Willie Welch took six for 52. Needing 200 to win the OHJs reached 187 for 8.

The following year – 1969 – a presentation was made to MA to mark 50 years of running the Week. This was noted by Christopher Martin-Jenkins in the 22 August issue of *The Cricketer* who wrote:

> The Old Hurst Johnian Cricket Week – the cricket week at Hurstpierpoint College in Sussex for old boys of the School – is, in the quality of participating sides, one of the best of the School "weeks." This year between August 2 and 9, matches were played against the Free Foresters, Romany, Eton Ramblers, Old Amplefordians, Old Rossallians, Stoics, Sussex Martlets and the Buccaneers.
>
> The 1969 Week has a special significance for Mr M.A. Pitcher (a suitable name) because it is exactly 50 years since he raised the initial sides in the very first O.J. Week of 1920. He has been organizing sides – the war years excepted – ever since. Small wonder that a Presentation was made to him this year to thank him for all his hard work.

The Free Foresters were beaten by 25 runs thanks to

five for 42 from Jenkin who then took five for 12 against Romany who were beaten by two wickets. The OHJs batted first against the Eton Ramblers. Dick Smart opened with George Hill and was fourth out, having made 85. Gordon Grantham then ran through the Ramblers batting to take six for 25 in 19 overs. The opposition were two men short and were assisted by two members of the College staff – Harry Maxwell who had captained Trinity College Dublin, and Hugh Thomas, a slow-left-arm bowler, who had played for Shropshire. Not only, it seems, were the Ramblers short of players, they were also short of bowling as Maxwell and Thomas bowled more than half the overs.

The Old Rossallians replaced Leicester Ivanhoe and won their first encounter against the OHJs. The Old Amplefordian game was drawn but the OHJs were only 16 runs short of their target of 204, having been 53 for 5 before Bob Schad and John Blacker added 116. Set 230 to win the Stoics were 79 for 8 before the last three batsmen got the total to 168 for 9. The Sussex Martlets lost by 20 runs with Colin Henderson taking six for 49. In a close finish the Buccaneers were beaten by four wickets, Guy Waller hitting a six off the third ball of the last over. Earlier Keith Jenkin and Roger Goodacre had given the OHJs a good start with a partnership of 136 for the first wicket.

It was during this summer that all three Cricket Wicket managers would have been seen on the North Field – MA, George Hill and Tom Moulton who had been born the previous January.

The 1970 Week was yet another one to be affected by rain. It began with a draw against the Free Foresters. It was a high-scoring game with 518 runs in the day. Thanks to an opening partnership of 144 by Keith Jenkin, 101, and Roger Goodacre, 49, followed by 60* from Bob Schad, the OHJs declared at 261 for 4. The Free Foresters finished five runs short of victory – Willie Welch five for 93 – with one wicket remaining. Both sides bowled 60 overs each.

In a low-scoring match Romany were defeated by 49 runs. On the following day the OHJs needed 224 to beat the

Eton Ramblers. Starting badly, they lost three wickets for seven runs and subsequently lost by 72 runs. Fortunes changed the following day when the Old Rossallians were beaten by eight-wickets. The visitors had reached 101 for 1 but an inspired spell by Keith Jenkin – six for 18 in 17 overs caused a collapse which reduced them to 155. Roger Goodacre, 49, and Dick Smart, 76* – saw the OHJs to an eight-wicket victory.

On Wednesday rain stopped the Old Amplefordian game after lunch but not before Nick Searls had scored 107 out of 177 in 93 minutes. The subsequent rain was bad enough to cause the cancellation of the Stoics match.

The weather improved on the Friday when the Sussex Martlets were beaten by 43 runs. This was Roger Goodacre's match – an unbeaten 101 and six for 33. Rain caused the abandonment of the Buccaneers match. Gwyn Hughes, formerly of Glamorgan and Cambridge University and Master in charge of Cricket at St Paul's School for 35 years, was top scorer with 33 out of a total of 184 made in 76.5 overs. The OHJs only used four bowlers with Dick Smart taking four for 47 in 30 overs and Keith Jenkin four for 83 in 27.5 overs.

The 1971 Week began well but rain ruined three of the last four games. The Free Foresters won by 62 runs after being dismissed for 144 despite the presence in their ranks of JRT Barclay who had just commenced his career with Sussex. OHJ David Pike was the architect of the OHJ collapse with figures of 19-12-19-7. This was followed by an eight-wicket win against Romany. The Eton Ramblers were two men short and were aided by Hugh Thomas, who joined the Duck Club, and Bruce Ruddock then a pupil in the College. The Ramblers had little answer to the bowling of Roger Hickman – also still at school – who took six for 59. The Old Rossallians, aided by the presence of RMO Cooke of Essex, declared at 185 for 8 but failed to capture the last OHJ wicket.

The Old Amplefordians were replaced by the Cryptics who declared at 181 for 7. Rain brought matters to an end shortly afterwards. Among the Cryptics were two future Headmasters – Christopher Saunders a Cambridge blue – Eastbourne and Lancing; and Tony Beadles – King's Bruton and Epsom. The rain brought the Stoics match to an end after only nine overs.

The weather was better on the following day when the Sussex Martlets were beaten by 34 runs. David Gibson of Surrey and now the College cricket coach scored 21 and then took three for 18 in 13 overs. Amongst his victims was John Barclay. Roger Hickman then took five for 57.

The rain brought the Buccaneers match to an early end, but not before Gwyn Hughes had produced the remarkable figures of nine for 6 in 16.5 overs, 12 of which were maidens. Dick Smart and David Gibson then reduced the Buccaneers to 31 for 5. Such are the vagaries of cricket that Gwyn Hughes was caught at the wicket for 0.

Only one match was won in 1972, although only one more wicket was needed with the Free Foresters still 28 runs away from victory and the Romany match was drawn with the scores level. Needing 257 the OHJs lost two quick wickets but a third wicket partnership of 214 – Roger Goodacre 92 and Bob Schad 118 – got them well on the way; however the quick loss of five more wickets frustrated their efforts. The Eton Ramblers won by 55 runs after declaring at 290 for 6.

On the following day, the OHJs, batting for 70.1 overs, did not make enough runs and the Old Rossallians made light of their task, winning by five wickets. The Cryptics won a low-scoring match by three wickets, but batting was easier on the Thursday when, against the Stoics, the OHJs declared at 271 for 4, Keith Jenkin and Roger Goodacre sharing an opening partnership of 133. Jenkin went on to 162 (out of 229 scored while he was at the wicket). This year Nagenda was wicketless, but he made 78 as the Stoics, making a valiant attempt to win, fell five runs short with the last pair at the wicket.

The Sussex Martlets declared at 233 for 8 with Dick Smart having taken five for 60. The OHJs made light of their task. This time Jenkin and Goodacre made 189 for the first wicket when Goodacre was lbw to Alan Wadey who was later to play for Sussex. Jenkin continued on his merry way making an unbeaten 158. He and David Gibson added 45 for the second wicket to take the OHJs to an eight-wicket victory. Such was Jenkin's dominance that the former Surrey all-rounder David Gibson only managed 8*.

Once again rain ruined the Saturday match against the Buccaneers. This year Gwyn Hughes was top-scorer with 54* as the Buccaneers made their way to 136 in 65.5 overs – Dick Smart taking four for 42 in 31 overs. Rain came soon after the OHJs began their reply.

The reports for this period tend to be rather brief, but we are told that Smart 'bowled his heart out'. It is appropriate therefore to set out his figures for the Week:

Opponent	Overs	Mdns	Runs	Wkts
Free Foresters	14	4	34	3
Romany	23	3	80	3
Eton Ramblers	25	7	67	1
Old Rossallians	21	5	70	3
Cryptics	15.1	4	45	2
The Stoics	18	0	79	4
Sussex Martlets	24	7	60	5
Buccaneers	31	13	42	4
Total	172.1	43	477	25

He bowled one wide and one no-ball.

Although no one knew it, 1972 was MA's last Cricket Week. He died on 7 May 1973.

Maurice Pitcher's contribution to OHJ cricket was immense and no one before or since has achieved more than he did. The superlatives run out very quickly and it seems best to reproduce the obituary notice which appeared in the summer issue of the *Hurst Johnian* in 1973:

Maurice Pitcher was the personification of loyalty. Many thousands of old boys have great affection for their school, but no one could possibly have devoted himself so whole-heartedly as M.A. did to Hurst. He showed the greatest interest in everything connected with the school, and he loved to visit it, but he will be remembered chiefly for his unswerving and selfless devotion to Hurst's cricket. He started the Cricket Week in 1920 and remained the manager for the rest of his life. His unbounded optimism and enthusiasm kept it going in hard times, and eventually he built up the fixture list to its present eminence, and he was known and respected by our many opponents just as he was by all O.Js who played in the "week". In those weeks he played well over a hundred innings and is only one of four players who have scored a thousand runs and taken a hundred wickets; but no figures can ever tell of the work which he did in fostering interest in O.J. cricket. He was never in too much of a hurry, but he was always busy; he always had a friendly word for the children even when they plagued him in the scorebox, where he took up his position when his playing days were over: he always had a new anecdote of days gone by: he was always full of thanks and appreciation for any small job done by someone else, but he never sought praise or reward for the mammoth task which he did so faithfully and efficiently year by year. No one ever heard him say an unkind word: I doubt if an unkind word was ever spoken against him.

M.A. will always be remembered as Mr Cricket Week, but this was not his only claim to lasting recognition. He was an expert on carriage clocks, and was held in high regard as a horologist. His generosity was a by-word, and his word was his bond... facts which were acknowledged throughout his profession.

He was captain, secretary and treasurer of the Old Hurst Johnian Association Football Club and kept a team in the Arthur Dunn Cup for at least eight years after the school changed to Rugby Football in 1925. He and his brother E.L. both played representative football for the Amateur Football Association.

But it is as Hurst's outstanding cricket ambassador that M.A. will always be remembered. We extend our deepest sympathy to Mrs Pitcher and to his sons Harvey and George, happy in the knowledge that the latter will be helping to carry on the great tradition which his father founded. The week of 1973 will be just the same, but it will be so different. We shall miss the flicker of white acknowledgement which came so unerringly from the scorer's window, but we shall be happy that M.A. will be with us in spirit.

Thus the succession passed seamlessly to George Hill.

Chapter Five
George Hill 1973 to 2004

George Hill was the ideal successor to MA. A boy at Hurst from 1945 to 1951, he had been Captain of the School and Captain of Cricket in 1950 and 1951. National Service delayed his Cricket Week debut until 1954 when he had been described as 'something of an unknown quantity'. After Cambridge he had joined the College staff and was currently Housemaster of Martlet. He had also been Assistant Manager since 1959 and was therefore fully immersed in the running of the Week.

Although 1973 was generally a good summer there were two wet days which caused the cancellation of the Romany and Eton Ramblers matches. The Free Foresters won by six wickets. The OHJs struggled to 125 – Willie Welch making 54 and Baddeley taking six for 54. The Free Foresters took their time in reaching their target with Keith Jenkin taking three for 39 in 14 overs.

After two blank days the Old Rossallians were beaten by 94 runs following an OHJ declaration at 216 for 8. Good all-round bowling dismissed the Old Rossallians for 120. The following day the Cryptics batted first and declared at 210 for 6. In reply the OHJs made 129. Andrew Gough scored 44 while FitzGerald took six for 42.

Run-getting was no easier against the Stoics who, needing only 132, won comfortably by six wickets and for whom John Wardle, son of the Yorkshire and England slow left-arm spinner Johnny Wardle, took five for 24. The next day was better. Thanks to Keith Jenkin, who scored 86, the OHJs made 192 against the Sussex Martlets. Dick Smart then took six for 43 as the OHJs won by 64 runs.

On the Saturday the batting failed again as the Buccaneers dismissed the OHJs for 112. The damage was done entirely by Stuart Rankin who, having got lost on the way, arrived late and thus did not take the field until eight overs had been bowled. Coming on first change, Rankin proceeded to run through the OHJ batting, taking ten for 31 in 19.1 overs, the best bowling performance by anyone in all OHJ cricket. After this performance his fiancée, who was watching him play cricket for the first time, asked him, 'Do you do this every time you play?' On their way to victory the Buccaneers lost three wickets – all taken by Dick Smart who had now taken 150 Cricket Week wickets.

In the winter of 1973/74 a scorebox was erected in memory of MA Pitcher. It was positioned on the north-eastern boundary of the North Field. The following inscription was placed on the front:

This scorebox was given by his many friends
as a memorial to
M.A. PITCHER
who founded the OHJ Cricket Week in 1920
and was its manager for over 50 years

Gifts came from many OJs, the School,
Free Foresters, Romany, Eton Ramblers,
Old Rossallians, Cryptics, Stoics,
Sussex Martlets, Buccaneers
Members of his family and many others

The scorebox may be seen clearly from most parts of the ground, but the south-westerly view for the scorers can make life very difficult in bright late afternoon and early evening sunshine as well as when there is a strong south-westerly wind. Nevertheless, it is far better positioned than its predecessor which was by the pavilion.

Encouraged by George Hill, a number of younger players were now starting to appear – Andrew Gough, John Goodacre and Jeremy Rawlins in particular. Although 1974 was one of the wet summers, the Week did not suffer any interruptions.

The Free Foresters match was drawn with the scores level. Thanks to David Gibson, who made 97, the OHJs were able to declare at 200 for 7. The Free Foresters began well, not losing a wicket until the score had reached 112, but Keith Jenkin then took seven for 54 which made for an exciting finish. This was followed by a nine wicket win against Romany who declared at 196 for 7. After the early loss of Roger Goodacre, Keith Jenkin (71*) and Willie Welch (106*) took the OHJs to victory with a partnership of 177.

It was different on the following day. The OHJs could only manage 160 against the Eton Ramblers. Of this total Roger Goodacre (62) and John Blacker (67) were responsible for 129. The Ramblers, for whom de Grey took seven for 41, made their way to a four-wicket win.

Against the Old Rossallians, Paul Ruddlesdin made 68 out of 182. Willie Welch then took six for 44 as the opposition struggled to 137 for 8. On the Wednesday Roger Goodacre made 97 against the Cryptics out of a total of 240 for 8 declared, JMC Watson having taken five for 38. At close of play the Cryptics were 205 for 7, DHM Dalrymple having scored 75. Only seven wickets fell in the Stoics match which the OHJs won by six wickets after the Stoics had declared at 165 for 3.

The Sussex Martlets were defeated by 112 runs. Batting first, the OHJs declared at 230 for 5, Bob Schad scoring 50 and Andrew Gough an unbeaten 77. The Martlets could only manage 117, having little answer to the off-spin of Keith Jenkin – five for 24 and Bill Baxter – three for 38. The Week ended with a drawn match against the Buccaneers in which nobody appears to have done anything with distinction.

After a poor start, 1975 became the sixth hottest summer of the century, bettered only by 1911, 1949, 1921, 1959 and 1947. The Week began with a 36-run win over the Free Foresters who had been set 211 to win. Keith Jenkin was the architect of victory, taking seven for 72 in 20 overs. The following day Romany made 184, but the OHJ batting was too good and a four-wicket victory came in only 46.4 overs – Roger Goodacre 55* and Paul Ruddlesdin 53* who, next day took five for 42 to help dismiss the Eton Ramblers for 155. He then scored an unbeaten 73 to steer the OHJs to a two-wicket win. The Old Rossallian game was drawn, but the OHJs were in a winning position when stumps were drawn needing only one more wicket with the Old Rossallians still 37 runs short.

On the Wednesday Nick Searls made 144 for the Cryptics who were then able to declare at 230 for 7. The OHJs managed to hold out for a draw, reaching 191 for 8. Against the Stoics the OHJs batted for 63 overs before declaring at 174 for 8. The Stoics reached 101 for 3 before proceeding to lose five wickets for 48 more runs and so the match ended as a draw.

The OHJs began well against the Sussex Martlets being able to declare at 215 for 3 after Andrew Gough and Keith Jenkin had shared an unbroken fourth wicket stand of 151. Another unbroken stand – this time 150 – by P Wreford and J Davies guided the Martlets to an eight- wicket win. This turned out to be the only defeat of the Week. On Saturday the OHJs made 169 in 74 overs. Willie Welch then took six for 29 as the Buccaneers collapsed for 71, thus losing by 98 runs.

George Hill left Hurstpierpoint College at the end of the Summer Term of 1975 to become Headmaster of Llandaff Cathedral School. As it was so far from Hurstpierpoint he did not feel that he would be able to continue as Manager and he therefore resigned. The Hurst Johnian Club Committee would have none of it and refused to accept his resignation. George agreed to continue but said that if he did so he would use his caravan and camp at the College.

The summer of 1976 was the best one of the 20th century. Following the hot and dry summer of 1975 and a very dry winter, the North Field – apart from the square – became a mass of dry brown grass. It was the 50th Week and the Romany game was treated as the celebratory match. It was also Charles Carr's 25th year as President of the Duck Club for which achievement he received a presentation.

That summer George Hill and Keith Jenkin parked their caravans on the edge of the North Field. Nothing was said by the College authorities, but the following year

Manyweathers – the field to the west of the North Field – was made available. Others soon followed the example set by the Hills and the Jenkins and either parked their caravans or pitched their tents on the field. It is an excellent site for campers as it has a very good view of the North Field and is a very safe place for small children. On one or two occasions in the past when Manyweathers was unavailable the campers had to move to Highfield – now an astroturf hockey pitch. This was never very satisfactory as it was rather cut off from the North Field.

The start of camping somewhat changed the nature of the Week as it gradually became more family-friendly. What had been a bachelor Week smoothly changed into one where women and children felt fully at home. This development is one of several reasons why the Week continues to flourish and to attract younger players.

The Week began with a two-wicket victory over the Free Foresters who, one man short, were dismissed for 181. In reply the OHJs subsided to 91 for 7, but George Pitcher, 41*, and George Hill with 43 came to the rescue. Hill left at 166. Dick Smart joined Pitcher and they scored the necessary runs. On the Sunday the batting failed against the Romany bowling, but Lee Herbert with 57* enabled the OHJs to declare at 177 for 7 – an effort which had taken 61 overs. Romany then raced to a nine-wicket victory in only 39.3 overs – F Patterson 83* and AJG Bewick 55*.

Against the Eton Ramblers the OHJs reached 193 for 3, only to lose their last seven wickets for 24 runs. The Ramblers then made their way to a four- wicket win. Another batting failure followed against the Old Rossallians. Needing 177 to win, the OHJs lost wickets at regular intervals and were all out for 96. On the following day the Cryptics became the next team to dispatch the OHJs for less than a hundred. The Cryptics declared at 187 for 8 and in reply the OHJs were soon 16 for 5, eventually struggling to 95.

On Thursday the OHJS made 156 for 8 declared against the Stoics. That the total reached 156 was entirely due to Bob Schad who made 56* and George Pitcher who was unbeaten on 70. The other six batsmen who went to the wicket all failed to get into double figures. The Stoics held out for a draw, reaching 121 for 9 with Derek Semmence, the former Sussex player who was now the College cricket coach and groundsman and who was making his Cricket Week debut, taking five for 44, after having been one of those to be dismissed in single figures.

The batting improved dramatically against the Sussex Martlets who were beaten by 22 runs. Batting first, the OHJs made 235 for 3 declared with Roger Goodacre unbeaten on 119. As so often Dick Smart then rose to the occasion taking six for 77 as the Martlets were dismissed for 213.

Sad to relate the batting failed again against the Buccaneers who won by 86 runs. The OHJs needed 206 but were all out for 119. Eight batmen were dismissed for single figures as Gwyn Hughes returned figures of 10.3-7-8-5. Since 1968 he had taken 33 OHJ wickets at a cost of 6.6.

Apart from the heat and the drought, 1976 was the year of the yellow hat which had to be worn by the last fielder to drop a catch. This lasted for a few matches before Bob Schad missed one. Given the hat, he responded with, 'I'm not wearing that stupid thing' and flung it on the ground. The hat has never been seen again. It only remains to be added that had the hat been in use in the 2018 Buccaneers match it would have been worn by nine people.

Although 1977 was a more normal type of English summer with a good amount of rain, only the Free Foresters match was affected. Aided by the presence of Michael Barford, the Free Foresters declared at 212 for 6. The OHJ innings was three balls old when the rain came but, unfortunately, Roger Goodacre had already been dismissed.

The Romany match was drawn with the scores level. Batting second, Romany had lost nine wickets with Clive Stiff having taken five for 52. No one made many runs against the Eton Ramblers who had a comfortable five wicket win. Willie Welch took five for 90 against the Old Rossallians who made 162. The OHJs took 64.2 overs to record an eight-wicket victory, Bob Schad leading the way with 55. On

Wednesday, needing 239 to record their first victory over the Cryptics, the OHJs finished eight runs short with three wickets in hand.

The Stoics, requiring only 123, won easily by eight wickets. On the following day the Sussex Martlets declared at 245 for 7. The OHJs used eight bowlers who between them sent down 61 overs of which Keith Jenkin bowled 20. No one got going for the OHJs who ended the day on 150 for 8. Gwyn Hughes did not appear for the Buccaneers who lost by 26 runs after the OHJs had declared at 226 for 7. The Buccaneers started well, but the middle order collapsed, and they were all out for 200.

The magazine reports in the 1970s tend to be very brief and in one or two instances are virtually non-existent. This mirrors other sports as well and the historian finds himself longing for the detailed match reports of the 19th and early 20th centuries. Fortunately, all the Cricket Week scorebooks have survived, and it is possible to work out what happened.

The 1978 Week provided some interesting cricket. The Free Foresters game was drawn. Roger Goodacre, 71, and Angus Stewart, 59, added 99 for the second wicket, but no one else did very much and after 72.4 overs the OHJs declared at 198 for 9. Dick Smart then dismissed the first three Free Forester batsmen by which point they were 5 for 3. They eventually reached 156 for 6, Michael Barford having made 66. Romany then won a low-scoring match by 24 runs. Heavy rain brought a 12-a-side-match against the Eton Ramblers to a premature end. Batting first the OHJS declared at 174 for 6 with Roger Goodacre unbeaten on 103. The Ramblers began their reply but after 3.1 overs the heavens opened.

The Old Rossallian game was a low and slow-scoring affair. The OHJs made 150, Andrew Gough 61. In reply the Old Rossallians reached 135 for 8. The rain then returned on the Wednesday after the Cryptics had made 66 for 4.

The next three games all produced exciting finishes. The Stoics won a very low-scoring game by 46 runs. They declared at 141 for 9, the innings having been held together by the former Surrey 2nd XI player AH Brown who made 84* as Derek Semmence bowled 19 overs to take six for 16. The OHJS started reasonably well and the score reached 93 for 4, but Cronkshaw, in his eleventh over, took four wickets in five balls and then took a further wicket with the second ball of his next over. His final figures were 12-5-19-5. Not to be outdone at the other end Nagenda took five for 42. In the final 2.2 overs the OHJ total had gone from 93 for 4 to 95 all-out.

After batting for 77 overs, of which Dick Smart and Kevin Rickard bowled 58, the Sussex Martlets declared at 201 for 4. This time Derek Semmence was playing for the opposition and made 103*. Consistent batting brought the OHJs to the last over needing three to win. Hayward had Searls stumped and two balls later dismissed Dick Smart. Colin Henderson blocked the next and then hit the fourth ball for four to win the match. This was the 50th match between the Sussex Martlets and the OHJs. To commemorate the occasion an oak tree was planted by the Armoury Path which runs between the North Field and Manyweathers.

There was another close finish to the Buccaneers match. Needing 167 to win the Buccaneers reached the start of the penultimate over requiring 12 runs with three wickets in hand. This was bowled by Smart in search of his 200th Cricket Week wicket. He was unsuccessful. Jenkin bowled the last over, took the eighth wicket and conceded four runs. The Buccaneers were six runs short.

The 1979 Week did not start very well. Batting first against the Free Foresters, the OHJs were 4 for 3 and then 26 for 6. That the total eventually reached 122 was due to an unbeaten 59 by Bill Baxter who was assisted by Kevin Rickard in an eighth wicket partnership of 52. The Free Foresters won, but not before they had lost eight wickets. Willie Welch took five for 42 against Romany who declared at 197 for 9. The OHJs began well, being 95 for 2 before wickets began to fall, and could only manage to reach 166 for 7. The Eton Ramblers match was drawn but Dick Smart took his 200th Cricket Week wicket while, to the apparent amazement of the younger players, George Hill bowled fifteen overs.

Rain reduced the Old Rossallian match to 35 overs each although there were no restrictions as to how many overs each bowler could bowl. Bob Cooke made 77 and the OHJs needed 162 but they lost their last wicket in the final over. Rain led to a late start in the match against the Cryptics who made 175. Chris Cowley made 40* but the OHJs could only reach 153 for 8.

The Stoics were beaten by 55 runs. Chasing 140, tight bowling by Willie Welch, Dick Smart, Robert Scull and Colin Henderson dismissed them for 84 – revenge for the previous year's disaster. A strong Sussex Martlets side with four first-class cricketers – Derek Semmence, John Denman and Ralph Cowan of Sussex, and Bob Gale of Middlesex who showed his class with an innings of 43 – won by three wickets. The Week ended with a victory over the Buccaneers who had declared at 210 for 5 with A Watts making 85 and AS Dixon 92. Paul Ruddlesdin with 65* and Willie Welch 45 saw the OHJs to a four-wicket win.

The Manager was delighted to report that 28 players had been available for selection. New young players were appearing. They were still able to stay in the school while those with young families were part of an ever-growing number of campers on Manyweathers.

The 1980 Week began with a high-scoring match against the Free Foresters. The OHJs declared at 256 for 2 – Roger Goodacre 116* and Keith Jenkin 65 – scored in 66 overs, but 53.2 overs later the Free Foresters had won by three wickets with David Stewart, a member of the College staff, making 52 out of an opening partnership of 83 before Prentis 64* and Barford 81* took the score from 131 for 3 to the required 257. The next day saw the only OHJ victory of the Week as Romany were beaten by 55 runs.

John Goodacre made a century before lunch against the Eton Ramblers. He was unbeaten on 122 when, with the likelihood of rain, the OHJs declared at 198 for 1. The rain arrived sooner than anticipated with the Eton Ramblers score at 10 for 1 in the fourth over. On the following day the OHJs could only manage 130 against the Old Rossallians who had little difficulty in winning by five wickets.

Against the Cryptics Paul Ruddlesdin made 91 out of a total of 194, but, although Keith Jenkin took five for 43, the Cryptics held out for a draw with numbers 9 and 10 at the wicket. On Thursday the Stoics made 218 with GF Bensly making 137 out of the 204 scored while he was at the wicket. Apart from Roger Goodacre who made 57 and Angus Stewart with 52, no one else could do much and the match ended in a draw. Another Derek Semmence century led to a Sussex Martlet declaration at 212 for 4. The OHJs struggled for runs and were well behind at the end. The Week finished with a heavy defeat by the Buccaneers who declared at 214 for 4 with PA Thompson undefeated on 109. Other than Roger Goodacre who made 46, no one could cope with the bowling of G Smith who took six for 22 as the OHJs collapsed for 75.

Apart from the early hours of Thursday when a thunderstorm led to the cancellation of the Stoics match, the Week of 1981 was blessed with some of the best weather of the entire summer and even though the ground was flooded on the Thursday, play started on time on the Friday.

There was a close finish on the first Saturday when the Free Foresters won by 5 runs. The OHJs only needed 166 but no one was able to stay with Roger Goodacre who opened and was ninth out and whose 63 was the highest score of the match. The Romany match, in which Keith Jenkin scored 79 and took five for 60, could have gone either way: at the close the OHJs needed one more wicket and Romany ten more runs.

The Eton Ramblers lost by 98 runs after the OHJs had made 219 for 7 - Paul Ruddlesdin unbeaten on 88. Keith Jenkin then took four for 46 in 13 overs. The Old Rossallians won by 46 runs having set the OHJs a target of 229. The OHJs never got going against Bob Cooke's leg breaks which gave him figures of seven for 61. The Cryptics match was yet another one to end with scores level: 200 and 200 for 9. A Cryptic run out in the last over did not help their cause.

There was another close finish in the Sussex Martlets game with the OHJs requiring one more wicket and the Martlets ten more runs. The Buccaneers won by nine wickets. They dismissed the OHJs for 159 with Collett taking five for 65. In reply Thompson and Dixon (103*) took the Buccaneers to 158 before Thompson was out for 58. A four from Dixon then gave him a century and the Buccaneers a nine-wicket victory.

The report of the Week's doings concluded with these words, 'Cricket Week is not just a cricket week – it is a social event.' Nearly forty years later this continues to be the case with the daily sherry session, the presence of ex-players, players, wives, girlfriends and children and OHJs. 1981 turned out to be Len Hitchcock's last season of umpiring. He was the first and, for a long time, the only Honorary Member of the Duck Club, and had umpired every Cricket Week match since 1967.

The report for 1982 began with these words, 'We had really hot weather and thoroughly enjoyed our stay in sunny Sussex.'

The Free Foresters won with nine balls to spare. Set 190 after an OHJ declaration the innings was held together by David Stewart who made 83. Earlier Keith Jenkin had made 57. Another fifty from Jenkin – 86 this time – enabled the OHJs to set Romany a target of 230 which turned out to be too much as they were all out for 176. The Eton Ramblers scored 284 for 8 declared with Dick Smart bowling 25 overs to take four for 105. The OHJs won with seven balls to spare – Roger Goodacre 111, Paul Ruddlesdin 57 and John Goodacre 59* – were the main contributors to the victory.

There have been a great many close finishes over the years, but one of the closest must be the Old Rossallian victory by two wickets with the winning run coming off the last ball of the match after Bob Cooke had made 97.

In the Cryptics game Dick Smart, who eventually bowled 28 overs, took four of the first five wickets to fall at which point the Cryptics total was 78 for 5. Two future Headmasters – Tony Beadles – King's School, Bruton and Mark Allbrook – Bloxham, who was a Cambridge University and Nottinghamshire off-spinner and was then on the Hurst staff, added 150 before a declaration at 228 for 5. The match ended with the OHJs needing 11 off the last over, but who only succeeded in scoring two runs and losing a wicket.

On the following day the Stoics won comfortably by eight wickets. Vanderstein took five for 32 to help dismiss the OHJs for 145 which was nowhere near enough. On the Friday Derek Semmence made another century for the Sussex Martlets who declared at 257 for 5, but defensive play by John Goodacre and Keith Jenkin achieved a draw. The OHJs ended on 143 for 7. This year the Buccaneers were defeated by six wickets after Chris Procter had taken four for 47.

To sum up in the words of the reporter, 'Every Week has its highlights. There were many in 1982.'

The first half of the Summer Term of 1983 was wet but as Common Entrance, O and A levels approached the weather changed for the better and the 1983 Week suffered nothing in the way of interruptions.

The first two matches were drawn but in both the result was in doubt up to the last over. Against the Free Foresters the OHJs began well – Roger Goodacre 58 and Paul Ruddlesdin 78 – but then lost quick wickets before declaring at 252 for 9. The Free Foresters started well with an opening partnership of 146 – WJ Wesson 74 and JRF Hardy 88 – but finished on 249 for 6. On the Sunday Romany declared at 223 for 8. The OHJs ended on 217 for 9. In a marathon bowling performance, A Bewick bowled unchanged for 26 overs, taking five for 98.

Borrowing John Bettridge and Chris Procter, the Eton Ramblers made 233 for 8 declared in 51 overs. Led by Bill Baxter, who scored 83, the OHJs cruised home to win by seven wickets with Robert Florey unbeaten on 55. There was a third close finish in the fourth match when the Old Rossallian game ended with the OHJs requiring one more wicket and the Old Rossallians holding out with Numbers 9 and 11 at the wicket, 27 runs short of victory. Keith Jenkin had figures of six for 71 in 22 overs.

The Cryptics won again – this time by five wickets. The OHJs could only muster 177 runs in 73 overs – Roger Goodacre top-scoring with 53. The Cryptics had little trouble in scoring the necessary runs even though Keith Jenkin took four of the five wickets that fell. The Stoics then won by 91 runs, having declared at 242 for 7 and Dick Smart having bowled 25 of the 52 overs to take three for 90. The OHJs reached 151 with Bob Schad top scoring with 51 and Cronkshaw taking four for 39. In a total of 259 for 7 declared, John Goodacre made 110 against the Sussex Martlets, sharing a 119-run fourth wicket partnership with Mark Allbrook who made 53, in a match which ended with the Martlets needing nine more runs with two wickets in hand.

The Buccaneers match was honoured by the presence of the South African Test player Russell Endean, who with his son Ross played regularly for Buccaneers. Wearing his faded South African cap, he was unbeaten for 11, having helped his son add 35 for the fifth wicket. The OHJs won the match by two wickets with little time to spare. At the time of writing Russell Endean is the last Test cricketer to appear in the Week.

The 1984 Week began with an eight-wicket win against the Free Foresters who set the OHJs a target of 256. With the total at 43 for 2, Peter Cockle was joined by Andrew Gough. In a splendid display of attacking cricket they added 216 runs – Cockle 104* and Gough 111* – taking the OHJs to an eight-wicket victory. This was the start of a purple patch for Gough as in the next game against Romany he scored an unbeaten 117 out of a total of 252 for 6 declared, Bewick having taken five for 78. Romany were never in a winning position, but rear order resistance prevented an

OHJ victory during which Richard Cooke, a member of the College staff, unwittingly joined the Duck Club. No one had told him that he was a candidate.

On the Monday Peter Stock took six for 85 to help dismiss the Eton Ramblers for 258 after a second wicket partnership of 145 between R Blewett, with 84, and W Robins, grandson of RWV Robins, who made 69. Scoring at 6.77 runs per over, the OHJs won by six wickets thanks to a partnership of 114 between Andrew Gough, 114* and Willie Welch 64*.

The OHJs had the better of a drawn match against the Old Rossallians. Although Andrew Gough's run of not-out centuries came to an end when he was caught by Tushingham off the bowling of Arundel for 32, the OHJs were able to declare at 229 for 6 and the Old Rossallians ended the day on 187 for 8. Against the Cryptics Dick Smart took six for 71 in 32 overs but the Cryptics recovered from 77 for 7 to reach 197 for 9 with DL Woodhead 101*. Apart from Martin Rose, who made 53, and Bill Baxter 32, no one else did very much and the OHJs were all out for 140, Sandy Ross having taken five for 57. Sadly, Gough only managed 4.

The Stoics match ended in a draw. Batting first the Stoics lost their first wicket at 90. The second wicket fell at 267 when D Foley had made 86. G Douglas was 121*. Despite Andrew Gough making 75, only Bill Baxter, 36, gave him any support and the OHJs could only manage 207 for 9. This was Gough's last appearance of the Week. His scores were as follows: -

111*	v	Free Foresters
117*	v	Romany
111*	v	Eton Ramblers
32	v	Old Rossallians
4	v	Cryptics
75	v	Stoics

This gave him a total for the Week of 453 runs at an average of 151.00 which is the highest individual number of runs scored in the Week. It was assumed by his fellow campers on Manyweathers that, judging by the mouth-watering odours emanating from his caravan, his record-breaking performance was entirely due to his wife' s cooking.

On the following day Mark Allbrook, four for 39, and Willie Welch, five for 31 routed the Sussex Martlets for 86 and the match ended in mid-afternoon with an eight-wicket OHJ victory. One of the wickets to fall was that of Bill Baxter who was out first ball. This turned out to be an event of considerable significance in the history of the Duck Club.

The Week ended with one of the great Cricket Week matches. There was no hint of the drama to follow when the Buccaneers declared, having set the OHJs a target of 218. Keith Jenkin and John Goodacre opened. Jenkin took strike only to be clean bowled first ball by Richard Gwynn whose next ball had Bill Baxter, whom it will be recalled had been dismissed first ball the previous day, caught by Thompson. Alistair Subba Row arrived at the wicket only to be bowled by Gwynn's next ball. Then came Graham Negus who played out the rest of the over. He and Goodacre took the score to 33 before he was caught off Gwynn for 8. David Procter made 2 before being caught. Kevin Rickard left when the score had reached 40.

All this time John Goodacre had stood firm amongst the wreckage of the innings and very slowly the tide began to turn. Guy Farnfield, who made 18, helped raise the score to 101. Willie Welch then became the fourth batsman to fail to trouble the scorers, but Dick Smart stayed while 63 were added for the ninth wicket at which point he became Gwynn's sixth victim. Wicketkeeper Jeremy Rawlins, who always batted at Number 11, arrived and, to the astonishment of all, he and Goodacre scored the necessary runs and, against all the odds the OHJs had won by one wicket. John Goodacre, the architect of victory was 152* and the valiant Rawlins was 2*.

This match is one of the best examples of the glorious uncertainties of cricket. As George Hill wrote in his 1984 report:

> At times our spectators left before the end of the game as they were 'petering out into tame draws'. This was

unwise for the wins against the Free Foresters, the Eton Ramblers and the Buccaneers were all achieved from unlikely situations.

There has never been any doubt in the minds of those who were present that the weather during the Cricket Week of 1985 was the worst ever, even more so than in 1939, 1951 and 1954, and that there has been nothing like it since. It began in rain and it ended with Neil Sayers and Robin Agate of the College groundstaff using the College tractor to tow several caravans off Manyweathers.

The Free Foresters match came to an end after 33 overs had been bowled in steadily worsening conditions. The Romany match was cancelled, and it rained for most of that day. The Eton Ramblers were unable to fulfil their fixture, so Derek Semmence gathered together a rather powerful eleven which contained three first-class cricketers – Harry Newton, Mark Allbrook and Derek himself – as well as Martin Speight, still a member of the school, who went on to play for Sussex, Durham and Wellington. On a wet wicket the OHJs found Mark Allbrook's off-spin a considerable problem as he took five for 33, including having Bill Baxter caught by Speight for a third consecutive golden duck, as they went down to a 94-run defeat.

The weather held on the Tuesday when the Old Rossallians made 241 for 7 declared – Chris Fryer 53 and Bob Cooke 70. Keith Jenkin then made 84 in an OHJ total of 225 for 7. After this the rain returned and the Cryptics game was called off. The weather relented for the Stoics match which ended in a draw. The OHJs made 212 – Martin Rose 90 – and the Stoics had reached 196 for 8 with Martin Cass having taken four for 41.

That, as it turned out, was the end. Yet more heavy rain led to the cancellation of the two remaining matches.

Dick Smart had the last word:

> We all had a great time despite the weather. The camping's the important thing.

After the trials and tribulations of 1985, the Week of 1986

was a considerable improvement. As George Hill put it:

Was it a good Week? The answer must be an unqualified 'Yes'

The wickets were very good – probably too good – and the side batting first never won. The three matches which ended in a definite result were won by the side batting second. Only once did a team lose all its wickets – OHJs against the Eton Ramblers. In the seven games which were played – the Romany match was cancelled because of the weather – only 88 wickets were taken out of a possible 140 and there were six declarations in the seven matches.

In the opening match against the Free Foresters Andrew Gough made 101 and the OHJs were able to declare at 233 for 7. By close of play the Free Foresters were 231 for 8 with David Stewart having made 78. The Romany match was rained off, but the weather recovered on the Monday when the Eton Ramblers won by seven wickets after dismissing the OHJs for 137. The Ramblers reached their target in 32.4 overs thanks to Matthew Fleming of Kent scoring 105*.

The Old Rossallians won by five wickets after an OHJ declaration at 263 for 8 – John Goodacre making 65 and Andrew Gough yet another century – 106 this time. However, with Bob Cooke leading the way with 60, the Old Rossallians won by five wickets in just 45.5 overs. After another OHJ declaration – 229 for 5 with Martin Rose scoring 59 and Guy Waller unbeaten on 78 – the Cryptics only needed 43 overs to win by five wickets.

The remaining three matches were drawn. Of these only the Stoics game came anywhere near being concluded. The OHJs needed 256 but apart from Peter Stock who made 86, four batsmen failed to score and two more were dismissed in single figures. It was left to Willie Welch and Tom Moulton to hold out for a draw as the OHJs clawed their way to 171 for 9. After 65 overs the Sussex Martlets declared at 246 for 4. Martin Rose made 119* and the OHJs reached 223 for 4 in 57 overs during which time Bill Baxter ended his run of first ball ducks by making 16. Thanks to 117 by Rob Rydon, the former Oxford blue, the Buccaneers were able to declare at 245 for 5. The OHJs made a bad start and were never in the hunt but thanks to 67* from Keith Jenkin were able to reach 191 for 7.

We are told that the Week saw the first appearances of Jonathan Rose, Justin Graham and Matthew Lowndes. Strangely, in view of what was to come, Tom Moulton's first appearance in the Week went unnoticed.

1987 was the fifth worst summer of the century but the Week was completed without interruption. The Free Foresters made 210 for 6 before declaring, but apart from Richard Cooke, who made 61, no one else really got going and the OHJs reached 183 with the last pair at the wicket. Although Keith Jenkin made 69 out of a total of 202 against Romany it was not enough to prevent a seven-wicket defeat.

The game against the Eton Ramblers on Monday 3 August is one of the most renowned matches in the OHJ cricketing canon. The OHJs batted first. Martin Rose made 106* and Clem Davey a belligerent 55 before Willie Welch declared at 219 for 6. The Ramblers began their reply. A Hughes-Onslow and W Robins had put on 107 for the first wicket before Hughes-Onslow was dismissed for 28. Scott, having made 3, left at 133. Robins, continuing to flog the bowling to all quarters of the field, and J Boden took the score to 203 for 2. An easy victory was clearly on the cards.

At this point, however, Willie Welch had Boden caught behind by John Bettridge – 203 for 3. Pettifer scored a single before being bowled by Dick Smart – 204 for 4. Nichols gave a catch to Angus Stewart off the bowling of Welch – 205 for 5. Smart struck again when Robins edged a catch to Bettridge to end a splendid innings of 141 – 205 for 6. The Ramblers were now in serious disarray as those who had not expected to be called upon to bat had now hurriedly to don pads and gloves to face an OHJ side that was scenting an unlikely victory. Stormont-Darling was the next to go – bowled by Smart for 0 - 205 for 7. Smart followed this up by getting Granville lbw for 0 - 205 for 8. In the next over Welch had Gibbs magnificently caught by

Martin Rose for 0 - 205 for 9. Two balls later he had Yelin caught by David Procter – 205 all out – and the OHJs had won by 14 runs. It was a highly spectacular collapse. The Eton Ramblers lost their last eight wickets for two runs in 25 balls with seven of them falling in 14 balls without a run being added. For the old firm of Smart – four for 23, and Welch – four for 41, this was their finest hour.

The OHJs were 98 for 5 against the Old Rossallians when Willie Welch 72* and Andrew Gough 45* had an unbroken partnership of 113 which led to a declaration at 211 for 5. The Old Rossallians then raced to a five-wicket victory with Tushingham to the fore unbeaten on 69. Set 264 by the Cryptics, the OHJs fell short by 24 runs, despite 109 from Andrew Gough and 56 from Matthew Lowndes. Thanks to 105 from Clem Davey and 57 from Andrew Gough the OHJs declared at 267 for 5 but were unable to dismiss the Stoics who were 234 for 8 when the game ended in a draw.

On the Friday Clem Davey made 54 out an OHJ total of 226 against the Sussex Martlets who, thanks to 115 from RG Davies who had played one match for Warwickshire, reached 174 for 1. A collapse then set in and the Martlets found themselves at 198 for 8. On the Saturday John Goodacre played for the Buccaneers and scored 70 out of a total of 243 for 8 declared. No one made very much for the OHJs who were defeated by 79 runs.

Having been in office since 1950 Charles Carr resigned as President of the Duck Club. In view of his three consecutive golden ducks Bill Baxter was universally regarded as the only possible successor – a position he still holds today.

The 1988 Week began with a three-wicket win against the Free Foresters who batted first and collapsed from 92 for 2 to 98 for 7, eventually reaching 123. Dick Smart did the damage, taking seven for 56 in 26 overs. The OHJs did not find batting any easier and took 60.1 overs to make the necessary runs with Bill Baxter beginning his Duck Club presidency with a duck.

Dick Smart was amongst the wickets again in the next match taking five for 40 against Romany who were all out for 240. Solid OHJ batting – Andrew Gough 53 and Paul Ruddlesdin 50* – ensured a six-wicket victory. Making up for their performance of the previous year, the Eton Ramblers won by four runs. Needing 227, the OHJs batted unevenly – 54 for 4 before Dave Procter with 77 and Paul Ruddlesdin with 66 took the score to 185 for 5. The score reached 217 for 6 at which point the last four wickets fell for five runs. This sequence included two run outs. On the following day Keith Jenkin's 88 out of an OHJ total of 247 was the one highlight of what turned out to be a rather uninteresting draw with the Old Rossallians who ended on 171 for 6.

Wednesday was a red-letter day as the OHJs beat the Cryptics for the first time. Will Pike made 54 as the OHJs reached 221. Mark Williams, batting at No.10 and making 41, was the only Cryptic to make any runs as Keith Jenkin took four for 87. Against the Stoics, Jonathan Rose made 61 and Bill Baxter an unbeaten 57 to set up an OHJ declaration at 207 for 7. It was, however, not enough to prevent a seven-wicket Stoics victory with Kates scoring 69 and Strange 56.

Despite the presence of three first-class cricketers in Simon Hoadley, Richard Davies and Derek Semmence, the Sussex Martlets took 77 overs to make 231 for 5. In reply Andrew Gough made 88 and Martin Rose 64*, but the OHJs found that making 232 in 52 overs was too much. The Week ended with a five-wicket defeat by the Buccaneers who dismissed the OHJs for 174. An unbeaten 84 by Rob Rydon took the Buccaneers to a five-wicket win in only 36.4 overs.

During the Week two milestones were overtaken. Dick Smart took his 300th wicket and Jeremy Rawlins now had more dismissals behind the stumps than John Neal.

1989 was the second-best summer of the century. It was recorded that on the first day George Pitcher 'was relieved when he did not have to respond to the call when the Free Foresters turned up one short'. The simple answer was to play ten-a-side. In the event the OHJs were all out in 37 overs for 136, Bill Baxter top-scoring with 35. The Free Foresters only needed 29.5 overs to win by seven wickets.

There had been problems with the fixture list and the Eton Ramblers therefore appeared on the Sunday. This was another low-scoring game. The OHJs could only manage 125 – W Nicholson taking six for 55. The Ramblers, however, were all out for 99, Roger Hickman taking four for 12 in ten overs. The Sussex Martlets came on the Monday and after J Barnes had made 97 declared at 225 for 6. Andrew Gough led the way with 82 but the OHJs lost by 9 runs.

Bob Cooke made 104* for the Old Rossallians who set the OHJs 262 to win. They faltered and were 132 for 6 before Chris Cowley and Dick Smart who made 66* managed to take the OHJ score to 231 for 6. As the Week went on the totals became larger, ranging from 283 for 2 to 200. The Cryptics led the way with the highest score of the Week. R Williams, 116, and RDN Topham, 107, put on 182 for the first wicket and then RK Sethi who had played for East Africa in 1975 made 44* before the declaration at 283 for 2. The OHJs were never in the hunt but eventually reached 213, largely thanks to Martin Cass who made 89. The Stoics declared at 233 for 5, A Fairweather having made 71, but consistent OHJ batting – Matthew Lowndes 51 and Rupert Hill 59 – took them to a four-wicket win.

There was no official match on the Friday but there were enough cricketers available for a match between the OHJs and the Duck Club President's XI. On the following day the Buccaneers, who needed 222 to win, were defeated by 21 runs largely thanks to Keith Jenkin who took six for 78. Earlier Willie Welch had made 67. There was one more game – Romany on the Sunday. This time George Pitcher did have to play as Romany were one short. This was Martin Cass's match – nine for 55 as Romany were dismissed for 118 in just 27 overs. Cass then top-scored with 37* and the OHJs moved a four-wicket victory.

There was subsequently much discussion about the desirability of a ninth game. It was ultimately decided to keep to the eight-fixture format. In 1990 the Free Foresters withdrew as they were finding it increasingly difficult to raise sides on Saturdays. This was mainly due to the development of country-wide league cricket which has been largely responsible for the decline in friendly and wandering cricket.

The 1990 summer was almost as good as that of 1989 so it was a pity that there were only six matches as a replacement for the Free Foresters had not been found and the Eton Ramblers had muddled their dates. The Week therefore began on the Sunday and Romany were beaten by five wickets. Romany batted for 69 overs before declaring at 195 for 6. In the OHJ reply Roger Goodacre was out first ball. Matthew Hastwell then completely dominated the proceedings with an unbeaten 134 which took the OHJs to a five-wicket win in only 36.2 overs. On Tuesday a Tushingham century – 103* – enabled the Old Rossallians to declare at 243 for 6. With one exception – Jonathan Rose with 60 – the OHJ batting failed and they were all out for 160. After his heroics on the Sunday Matthew Hastwell was out first ball and thus joined the Duck Club.

On the following day a strong batting line-up could only manage 182 against the Cryptics. This total would have been even smaller had it not been for a partnership between Matthew Barry, number 10, and Ian Buckeridge, number 11, who added 61 for the tenth wicket. The Cryptics then proceeded to lose only one wicket, thanks to Mark Williams with 82* and J Boddington who also scored 82*. Andrew Gough made 116* against the Stoics who were set a target of 229 which they reached on the fifth ball of the last over, R Kinsella having made 95* and Israel 59*.

Consistent batting meant that the OHJs were able to set the Sussex Martlets a target of 269. The presence of Justin Mackrory, a member of the College staff who had played for Natal and who made 77, failed to prevent an 8-run OHJ victory. The Week ended with a 70-run defeat by the Buccanerers who, thanks to Rob Rydon with 80, declared at 233 for 7. The OHJs got off to a bad start – Roger Goodacre was again out first ball – and at one point were 16 for 5. Ed Welch with 40 and Matthew Heath with 46 achieved some respectability as the OHJs eventually reached 156 with Rob

Rydon having taken five for 42.

Despite the four defeats there were plenty of players available, but George Hill said in his report that 'It was quite difficult to balance the strength of the side while ensuring that everyone had a fair share of the cricket.'

The Week of 1991 saw the first appearance of the South Wales Hunts who became the Monday opponents. The Eton Ramblers, having moved to the first Saturday, were all out for 117 owing a great deal to J Boden who made 77. Only one other player – E Miles – made it into double figures. Strangely the OHJs used seven bowlers to bowl the 43.5 overs needed to dismiss the Ramblers who also sent down 43.5 overs as the OHJs moved to a seven-wicket win. The Romany match was a high-scoring one which ended in a draw. Only nine wickets fell in the day, Romany making 245 for 6 – J Skinner 101 – and the OHJs 233 for 3 – Andrew Gough 102 and Matthew Lowndes 81.

Captained by Jeremy Rawlins, the South Wales Hunts won by 154 runs after declaring at 264 for 8. The OHJs collapsed to 110 all out, Anthony Alexander taking four for 30 and G Meggitt four for 19. On the following day the OHJs – 137 for 9 – just managed to avoid being defeated by the Old Rossallians who had declared at 203 for 8. The OHJs then had the Cryptics at 145 for 7 before an unbroken eighth wicket partnership of 75 between Mark Williams and R Williams, 127*, allowed them to declare at 220 for 7. Only Hamish Reid, who scored 53, made any runs as the OHJs were dismissed for 141.

The Stoics were beaten by one wicket having set the OHJs 188 to win. The OHJs batted very unevenly, six players being dismissed for single figures, but Rupert Hill made 46 and, eventually, the last pair of King and Rawlins scored the last 17 runs. On the Friday Derek Semmence made 60 for the Sussex Martlets who declared at 208 for 7. Paul Ruddlesdin, 78, and Matthew Hastwell, 51, were the main architects of a four wicket OHJ victory.

Rob Rydon made another century, 100*, and Tim Mynott 52 for the Buccaneers who declared at 269 for 3. Although

Ed Welch made 120 the OHJs ended on 233 for 7. This was Keith Jenkin's last Cricket Week match. He was captain, bowled 15 overs and took one for 53, but was bowled by Rydon for 2. To mark the occasion the Buccaneers provided champagne at the wicket and a cake in the shape of a cricket bat in the pavilion. In 151 matches since 1952 he had scored 5232 runs at an average of 37.10 and taken 325 wickets at a cost of 18.22. His highest score was 162 and his best bowling performance was eight for 19.

It was around this time that the 12.30 Sherry Session developed into one of the major features of the Week. Beer and soft drinks have always been available in the pavilion, but there were those, notably George Pitcher and Hugh Thomas, who much preferred a pre-lunch glass or two of sherry. This developed into a small and somewhat select group of sherry drinkers but which soon expanded considerably. In an age when most thought that sherry drinking was on the wane the 12.30 glass of sherry by the pavilion became an extremely popular event. The start of the session is opened by the Grand Sherry Master sounding the sherry bell, usually coinciding with a drinks interval on the field of play. It should also be recorded that the scorers are not forgotten.

In 1992 the Eton Ramblers fixture fell through and so a match was played against the Mad Hatters who, as befitted their name, wore a variety of exotic headgear and who were beaten by eight wickets in what turned out to be the only OHJ victory in the Week. The Mad Hatters made 135. The OHJs raced to victory or at least Andrew Gough did. He came to the wicket with the score at 67 for 2. By the time the OHJs had won his score was 67. Meanwhile Matt Lowndes, his partner, was 6*.

On Sunday Romany declared at 336 for 4 which only took 54 overs. E Horne, 101, and J Skinner, 98, put on 182 for the first wicket after which Ward scored 70. The OHJ bowling took a fearful hammering: Matthew Hastwell went for 107 in 14 overs, Roger Hickman 56 in nine and Patrick McGahan 34 in five. Hastwell, however, had his revenge by scoring 122 out of the OHJ total of 250.

Roger Hickman took five for 62 as the South Wales Hunts made 229 for 9 declared with J Pritchard scoring 61. A late declaration – the OHJs had bowled 73 overs – meant that the clock was always a problem and the OHJs were 188 for 7 at the close. In what became a low scoring match against the Old Rossallians the OHJs struggled to 162 in 73.2 overs. In contrast the Old Rossallians fairly galloped to victory in only 38.4 overs. NH Crust made 68 and PH Tushingham, who always liked batting at Hurst, made 54.

A strong Cryptic side, which included Mark Alban, a Cambridge blue and nephew of Bill Alban who was on the Hurst staff from 1949 to 1982, reached 301 for 2. G Reynolds, 96, and I Wood, 109*, had an opening partnership of 166 after which A McEwan made 52. Only Gareth Dexter with 61 contributed much to the OHJ total of 157 and the Cryptics won by 144 runs. On Thursday Mark Semmence made 84 out of 238 for 6 against the Stoics who eventually won by four wickets, largely thanks to an opening partnership of 132 by T Braine, 61, and C Shoesmith, 78.

There was another high-scoring match on the Friday which ended with the Sussex Martlets needing three more runs and the OHJs three more wickets. Ben Drake, in one of his only two appearances in the Week, made 96 out of an OHJ total of 282 for 9 declared. The Martlets recovered from 11 for 2 due to a third wicket partnership of 112 between Derek Semmence, 103, and C Dare, 44. Mike Howard then knocked up 77, but steady OHJ bowling led by Dick Smart – four for 45 – kept matters under control which was helped by a run out when the Martlets were three runs short of victory. The Week ended with a 112 run defeat by the Buccaneers who, thanks to Close 55, Rob Rydon 64 and Tim Mynott 78, were able to declare at 240 for 6. The OHJs collapsed for 128. Only Peter Cockle, who made 40, and Roger Hickman 26* managed to get into double figures as J Downing took five for 29.

Five matches were lost and the main OHJ problem was the

inability to dismiss a complete side. Only the Mad Hatters lost all ten wickets. The OHJs could only take 38 out of 70 possible wickets whereas the opposing sides captured 64 OHJ wickets. The only way to win a match, it seemed, was to win the toss, field first, wait for a declaration and then trust to your batsmen to knock off the runs. An admirable idea, but it does not always work.

The Eton Ramblers returned in 1993. The match ended in a draw after they had declared at 281 for 9 with C Birch-Reynoldson having made 116. The OHJs began well with Hamish Reid and Peter Riddy making 42 but the middle order failed, and the day ended with the OHJs at 208 for 8. Matthew Hastwell scored 121 out of 226 against Romany for whom Simon Daniels, a former Glamorgan player, took five for 19. Romany went on to win by three wickets with Skinner scoring 50 and B Ward 57*.

The South Wales Hunts declared at 209 for 6 and this time the OHJ batting came off. Mark Semmence, 102, and Ed Welch, 70, made 153 for the first wicket and the game was won by eight wickets with time to spare to give the OHJs their first victory over the South Wales Hunts. Thanks to 115 from PH Tushingham (again) the Old Rossallians won by four wickets after the OHJs had declared at 252 for 6. Steady bowling by Matthew Barry – four for 59 – meant that the Cryptics could only make 207. Mark Semmence, 111*, and Ed Welch, 53, helped the OHJs to a well-deserved eight-wicket victory. The OHJs then made 222 against the Stoics who were 198 for 9 at the close.

The OHJs then had the better of a drawn game against the Sussex Martlets. The OHJs declared at 293 for 3, Hastwell, 147*, and Simon Cross, 81, having added 142 for the third wicket. The Martlets were never in the hunt and were 211 for 9 at the close. I Thwaites scored 104 for the Buccaneers who declared at 263 for 9. The OHJs were soon 36 for 6 and only a seventh wicket partnership of 75 between Matt Lowndes and Stuart Hall gave any respectability to the OHJ total of 124. Tim Mynott had figures of six for 25.

In conclusion George Hill noted that it had been a good

Week and that it was encouraging to see a good number of recent leavers appearing. Reference was also made to the effrontery of Ed Welch in hitting a six which had landed on the Manager's car.

In 1994 the wickets were so good that yet again run scoring was very high. Although the OHJs lost all ten wickets on three occasions they never managed to dismiss an entire team. In fact, they only took 54 out of a possible 80 wickets which cost 30.68 runs each. OHJ wickets, on the other hand, cost 27.20. Overall 3369 runs were scored for the loss of 117 wickets at an average of 28.79 each.

The Eton Ramblers game was lost. Thanks to Peter Riddy, 74, and Derek Semmence, 60*, the OHJs declared at 244 for 7. The Ramblers proceeded to win by two wickets with their opener G Dunning scoring 129. On the following day against Romany, Mark Semmence having made 95 and Simon Cross an undefeated 66, the OHJs finally declared at 271 for 5. Romany, however, managed to hold out for a draw having lost nine wickets in reaching 200. Roger Hickman took six for 41.

The South Wales Hunts match was a high-scoring draw. The OHJs batted for 62 overs before declaring at 262 for 6. Matt Lowndes made 53 and Nick Searls, rolling back the years, remained unbeaten on 53. In a typical Cricket Week finish the Hunts finished seven runs short of victory but with only two wickets remaining. It should be noted that W Taylor, 56*, and M Campbell, 2*, added 52 for the ninth wicket. On Wednesday the Cryptics won by seven wickets. The OHJs could only manage 175 – Matthew Hastwell making 73, while P Sullivan took six for 45.

The Stoics batted first and were soon 20 for 2, but R Smith, 152*, and S Goldie, 90, proceeded to add 233 for the third wicket. They declared at 291 for 3. The OHJs just managed to hold out for a draw being 224 for 9 at close of play. On Friday the Sussex Martlets dismissed the OHJs for 179, 104 of which were scored by Ed Welch, 64, and Stuart Hall, 40. The Martlets eventually won by three wickets. They started well with M Stevens making 90, but then made life rather difficult for themselves when the score went from 153 for 3 to 159 for 7.

This match is probably better known for what became known as the The Gray Affair. Chris Gray, a member of the College staff was playing for the Sussex Martlets and was therefore a Duck Cub candidate. George Hill had this to say about the Affair:

> The scorebook will show that he scored one run, but was it a run, or a leg bye? Did the umpire, in the excitement of a scrambled single and near run out fail to signal the leg bye? Should he or his colleague have changed the record after the innings was completed? Is Chris Gray a new category in the Duck Club... a lame duck? Who knows? But it was a very close run thing.

The Buccaneers match began with the OHJs being dismissed for 91. It might have been thought that the Buccaneers were in for a comfortable win. They did win, but as a result of an heroic performance by Matthew Hastwell, who took seven for 33 in 20 overs, they had managed to lose eight wickets by the time the score had reached 71. Spackman and Liston saw them home. In complete contrast to the other games in the Week this match lasted 84 overs in which 18 wickets fell for 186 runs. The highest individual score was 29 and 13 batsmen failed to get into double figures.

The 1995 Cricket Week began with a 56 - run victory against the Eton Ramblers who inserted the OHJs. Thanks to 100 from Ed Welch and 81 from Matthew Hastwell the OHJs made 252 with S Strickland taking five for 59. The Ramblers began well - G Dunning making 55, but they lost wickets steadily - Dick Smart four for 42 - and were all out for 196. On Sunday a very powerful Romany side declared at 297 for 3 after J Skinner, 106, and A Bragg, 133, had put on 155 for the first wicket. The Welchs, Willie with 44 and Ed who made 52, scored 96 out of the 136 runs off the bat (extras amounted to 15) which was all that the OHJs could manage as they went down to a 146 run defeat with Simon Daniels taking four for 15. In an extremely uneven overall batting performance, it was left to the OHJ tenth wicket pair of Willie Welch and Patrick McGahan to take the score from 99 for to 151 all out.

Matters improved on the Monday when the South Wales Hunts were defeated by seven wickets. Facing seven bowlers the Hunts were dismissed for 184. Mark Semmence, 103*, and Matthew Hastwell, 63, made batting look easy as the OHJS knocked off the runs at a rate of just under five runs an over. The boot was on the other foot on the Tuesday as the Old Rossallians only needed 27.1 overs to rout the OHJs for 94 of which Ed Welch made 31 and Extras contributed 24. At one point the Old Rossallians were 29 for 4 but only lost one more wicket on their way to victory.

Mark Williams made 58 and T Kidson 62 as the Cryptics made their way to 250 for 9 declared. The OHJs found runs hard to come by and had only reached 181 for 7 by the close of play, Matthew Hastwell unbeaten on 83. On Thursday the Stoics arrived three men short, so Paul Juniper who made 55, Hamish Reid who kept wicket and Stuart Hall helped out. Largely thanks to Juniper the Stoics made 186. In reply Peter Riddy was out for 12. Aaron Scoones 53*, and Mark Semmence 119*, then took the OHJs to a nine-wicket victory. The Sussex Martlets batted for 64.2 overs before declaring at 182 for 9, Derek Semmence having made 77. The OHJs only had 42 overs and could only reach 152 for 8, Mark Semmence 73*.

Batting first against the Buccaneers, the OHJs declared at 299 for 4. Ed Welch made 135, and Hamish Reid 94. The Buccaneers, borrowing John Bettridge, John Redford, Rob Willsdon and Tom Moulton who scored 30, were all out for 229. Another OHJ, Chunky Goulstone was the Buccaneer captain which meant that sixteen of the twenty-two players were OHJs.

By the end of the Week in which 34 players were available for selection, Dick Smart had taken his tally of wickets to 350 and seventy-five consecutive matches had been played without being rained off – a far cry from the 50s and 60s.

In the 1996 Week 30 players, amongst whom were Simon Warrender and Mike Harrison making their Cricket Week debuts, were available – very different from pre-war days. The increased player availability was very welcome, but it posed selection problems. It was difficult to give everyone a decent number of matches especially as there were those who could only manage one or two days. As has already been noticed the development of league cricket tended to reduce player availability on the two Saturdays. It was also not very easy to select a properly balanced side as there was now an expectation that everyone would be given a chance with either bat or ball, and it is a sad fact that some had come for a few games but never returned when they found themselves in the lower reaches of the batting order and were not called upon to bowl.

The Manager found himself having to umpire in the Eton Ramblers match as Arthur James who had taken over as umpire from Len Hitchcock had died suddenly in June. The Arthur James Shield for an outstanding performance in the Week is awarded in his memory. Jack Riddy made 69 and Matthew Hastwell 84 which enabled the OHJs to declare at 248 for 5. After going without a win for 11 matches the OHJs won by 25 runs.

Romany began with an opening partnership of 148 between J Skinner, 76, and M Russell-Vick, 81, but they then steadily lost wickets and were all out for 254. The OHJs struggled to 172 for 8 with Russell-Vick, who was having a good day, taking five for 69. On Monday the OHJs got off to a bad start against the South Wales Hunts, losing their first five wickets for 18 runs. Simon Parkinson and Lee Atkins staged a recovery and took the score to 76 before Parkinson was out. Atkins continued to hit and with the help of Stuart Hall and Ben Green – a future Chief Executive of Kent – managed to raise the score to 140. When the South Wales Hunts went in needing 141 David Ricketts scored an unbeaten 103 to achieve an eight-wicket victory.

Bob Cooke made 70* for the Old Rossallians who declared at 213 for 6. The OHJs never really looked like winning and were all out for 196. The Cryptics then administered a heavy defeat on the Wednesday. They declared at 225 for

2 – Mark Williams 84 and R Arscott 60*. Siviter then took six for 53 as the OHJs were dismissed for 99.

The Stoics did not need to borrow any players this year but found themselves dismissed for 97 in 33 overs after the OHJs had embarrassed themselves by taking the field with 12 men. Whether or not the OHJ captain's reaction to this was the same as that of Keith Miller when he was told that his New South Wales team was walking out to field with twelve men is not recorded. The OHJs lost five wickets on their way to victory.

After 81 Cricket Week matches without any interference from the weather, rain caused the abandonment of the Sussex Martlets game with the OHJ score at 124 for 1 (Hastwell 52*) in reply to the Martlet total of 192. As a result of the rain the Buccaneers match started late. The OHJs who had been sent in to bat declared at 183 for 5 with Mark Semmence unbeaten on 85. Good OHJ bowling ensured a steady fall of wickets as the Buccaneers were defeated by 70 runs.

1997 was George Hill's 25th season as Manager, an event which was marked by the presentation of a claret jug. For once the weather was poor. Both the Romany and Cryptics games were abandoned and the Stoics match started late.

The Eton Ramblers match was a low-scoring affair, but in typical Cricket Week fashion ended with all four results possible. The OHJs made 194 and, with one ball of the last over remaining, the Ramblers with nine wickets down needed six runs but could only manage a four. On Sunday Romany were 182 for 4 with M Drage 71* when the rain brought proceedings to an end.

The South Wales Hunts match was yet another match with a close finish. The OHJs declared at 182 for 8 after the 70-year-old Bob Schad had been the second highest scorer with 26. Peter Riddy then took five for 68, but with 74 from Dave Ricketts, the Hunts won by two wickets with three balls to spare.

On Tuesday the Old Rossallians were defeated for the

first time since 1977. Set 195 to win the OHJs won by six wickets, as Aaron Scoones, opening the batting, scored an unbeaten 101*.

The rain returned with a vengeance on Wednesday when the Cryptics match came to an abrupt end after 4.4 overs. So much rain fell that the Stoics match on the following day started late. The Stoics declared at 189 for 4, C Stayers having scored 75. Apart from Hastwell who scored 53, the OHJs could only manage 150 for 8 in reply. The batting improved on the following day against the Sussex Martlets. Thanks to Ed Welch with 67 and Simon May who scored 52, the OHJs declared at 265 for 7. Aaron Scoones then took four for 21 as the Martlets struggled to 167 for 6. The Week ended with a 57-run victory over the Buccaneers. The OHJs declared at 217 for 7 – Mark Semmence 66 – and Hastwell then took seven for 46 in 16 overs as the Buccaneers were all out for 160 – Lawes 52 – which gave the OHJs a win by 57 runs.

Five matches were won in 1998, one was drawn, and one was abandoned. There was only one defeat and that was by five runs. This was the best set of results since 1969.

The abandoned match was that against the Eton Ramblers which came to an end in the early afternoon at which point the OHJs had struggled to 122 for 8 in 41 overs. Romany had difficulty in raising a side and borrowed Jack Riddy, James Hall, Rupert Hill, Roger Hickman and Bob Schad. Despite these reinforcements they only managed to make 120. The OHJs, scoring at over five runs an over, won by eight wickets with Ed Welch leading the way with 73. The South Wales Hunts match produced another victory – this time by six wickets. The Hunts declared at 192 for 8. Simon Warrender 60, and Lee Atkins, 82, made 134 for the first wicket and the target of 192 was soon reached. On the following day Dick Smart took five for 49 to help dismiss the Old Rossallians for 145. The OHJs proceeded to win by six wickets with Lee Atkins undefeated on 62.

The winning streak came to an end on the Wednesday when the Cryptics won by five runs. The Cryptics, for whom J Coburn scored 78, the only substantial innings of the day, were all out for 172. At one point the OHJs were 38 for 5 so getting to 167 was not bad going. S Engelen took seven for 55. The following day saw the arrival of the Stoics three players and an umpire short. Ben Searls, David Hook and the 71 year-old Bob Schad completed the side and the author forsook the score box to don the white coat. The Stoics declared at 226 for 8, but it was not enough as the OHJs won by seven wickets with Aaron Scoones scoring 54 and Mark Semmence 114*.

The Sussex Martlets game was drawn. J Wills made 87* and Lee Atkins 93. The Martlets declared at 273 for 6, Mike Harrison taking four for 54. The OHJs pushed hard for victory and at close of play were 260 for 7, Hastwell having made 69 and Ed Welch 76*. The Week ended with another victory as the Buccaneers were defeated by six wickets. Using eight bowlers the OHJs dismissed the Buccaneers for 221, D Bray making 79. Again Welch 81 and Hastwell 66* dominated with the bat to secure a four-wicket victory.

The Week of 1999 was favoured by excellent weather. The match against the Eton Ramblers which produced 528 and 13 wickets, predictably ended in a draw. Jack Riddy 74, and Ed Welch 84, began with an opening partnership of 127. Matthew Hastwell arrived with the score at 131 for 2 and proceeded to score an unbeaten hundred. Needing 302 the Ramblers reached 227 for 9 with opener J Scobie making 90*. The OHJs used ten bowlers – only wicketkeeper Paul Atkins not bowling.

The Romany game was won by 85 runs. Thanks to Bill Baxter with 73 and Simon May who made 54, the OHJs were able to declare at 272 for 6. Romany were then dismissed for 187 with Stuart Hall taking four for 44 and Mark Semmence four for 72. On Monday David Ricketts made 97 which enabled the South Wales Hunts to declare at 237 for 6, Stuart Hall having taken four for 50. The OHJs began badly, recovered, and then collapsed to 213 all out, Ricketts following up his batting with five for 45.

For the Old Rossallians N Dixon had made 58* when they

declared at 195 for 7. The OHJs lost wickets steadily and were 112 for 7 when Hastwell and Harun Cordan joined forces and took the score to 185 when Hastwell was dismissed for 69. The ninth wicket went at 189 and Cordan and Smart could only acquire two of the seven runs required for victory and so the Old Rossallians won by five runs.

The Cryptics, having been inserted, declared at 199 for 8. A McEwan scored 73 and Aaron Scoones took four for 62. The OHJ batting was inconsistent with seven players failing to reach double figures and of those that did, no one made very much as the Cryptics won by 60 runs. A much stronger Stoics side won by two wickets in a match which only lasted for 60.3 overs. The OHJs batted first and were 86 for 9 when tail-enders Patrick McGahan and Jeremy Rawlins joined forces and added 17 for the tenth wicket. It is unfortunate to have to record that Extras was top scorer with 17. The Stoics knocked off the runs in 17.4 overs with J Kumar scoring 60.

Jonathan Pilgrim took five for 49 to help dismiss the Sussex Martlets for 174, D Peacock having made 68. At one point the OHJs were 95 for 5 but the lower order held things together and they scraped home by two wickets. The Buccaneers match was drawn. John Goodacre scored another century as the OHJs declared at 262 for 6, but were unable to dismiss the Buccaneers who struggled to 167 for 7.

In 2000 the bat did not dominate as much as it had done in previous Weeks. On the Saturday the Eton Ramblers made 205, G Dunning having made 52. C Huntington then took six for 24 as the OHJs struggled to 166, Matthew Hastwell top-scoring with 63. Most of the batsmen failed, seven being unable to reach double figures whereas Extras contributed 30. The following day saw the dismissal of Romany for 177 with O Youll scoring 75 and Peter Riddy taking five for 55. Mark Semmence, sharing an unbroken second wicket stand of 161 with Aaron Scoones, scored an unbeaten 107 as the OHJs won by nine wickets.

Semmence was in the runs again – 112 – on the Monday against the South Wales Hunts when he and Matthew Hastwell – 103 – added 224 for the third wicket as the OHJs made 242 for 4 declared. The Hunts could only manage 189 with M Phillips scoring 53 and the 73-year-old Bob Schad taking three for 51 in his last appearance in the Week. A deluge on Tuesday brought proceedings to a premature end when the Old Rossallians had reached 138 for 3, Jonty Arundel having made 60.

This was the year of the Millennium Festival for Wandering Clubs at Oxford in which the Cryptics took part and thus found themselves unable to play the OHJs. The South Wales Hunts, by contrast, managed to do both.

The Stoics match was another low-scoring affair. The OHJs were all out for 153 and eventually lost by two wickets. On the Friday the Sussex Martlets declared at 227 for 8 – Derek Semmence making 71 and N Beechey 68. The OHJs were soon 6 for 2, but then recovered to 95 for 3; however wickets then fell steadily and at the close of play they were 167 for 9. The Week ended with an eight-wicket defeat by the Buccaneers who, having bowled out the OHJs for 93, needed only 18.4 overs to win by eight wickets, P Hobcroft making 50*.

It was not the greatest of Weeks as far as performances went but plenty of players were available. It was also the year of the double-decker bus which accommodated the McGahan family for the entire week. As George Hill wrote, 'The Week is truly a family affair'. This was accentuated by the arrival of William Moulton on the first Saturday. News of his birth reached the rest of the Moulton family with his grandfather in the scorebox coping with the start of the last twenty overs.

The weather for the Week of 2001 was described as 'a total mixture.' Rain caused the cancellation of the Old Rossallians and Stoics matches. Fortunately, the other six matches produced a lot of good cricket. This was the first year of the electronic scoreboard which made life a great deal easier for the scorers who no longer had to deal with faulty and temperamental equipment which often involved precarious ladder work at the same time as keeping the score book going.

The account in the Hurst Johnian Club Newsletter tells us that the Eton Ramblers match was 'lost rather tamely'. At one point the Ramblers were 126 for 9 but a last wicket partnership of 67 took them to 193, J Scobie making 55*. In reply Stuart Hall scored 58 but the rest of the team kept losing their wickets and the OHJs lost by 33 runs. On the following day Romany declared at 231 for 8, Hastwell having taken four for 15. The OHJs, however, did not score quickly enough and frustratingly finished five runs short of victory, with three wickets in hand. The OHJs got off to a good start against the South Wales Hunts with Ed Welch making 97 as the OHJs reached 187 for 4, but the last wickets could only add another 30 runs as G Wallwork took five for 38. David Ricketts made 81 but the middle and lower order contributed little and the Hunts could only reach 193 for 8.

Tuesday's rain led to a late start to the Wednesday game against the Cryptics who declared at 156 for 9, Mike Harrison taking five for 44. The OHJs started badly – 3 for 1, 7 for 2, 9 for 3, 12 for 4, 17 for 5 and 29 for 6 before Hastwell steadied the ship with an unbeaten 53. By close of play the score had risen to 115 for 8.

Further rain on Thursday did not affect the start of the Sussex Martlets match on the Friday. The OHJs batted first and declared at 226 for 7 with Simon May making 57 and Hastwell 53*. The declaration was on the late side and in the event the Martlets struggled to 106 for 7 in 41 overs. The last match of the Week saw an easy victory over the Buccaneers who only managed 163 in 61 overs. Thanks to an innings of 103* by Mark Semmence the OHJs eased themselves to a seven wicket win in just 32.3 overs.

The Week of 2002 did not get off to the best of starts. The Eton Ramblers found themselves unable to raise a team and although there were enough OHJs available to make up two teams for what might be described as an internal match, it was not the real thing. It did not help that rain on the following day caused the abandonment of the Romany match after 24 overs.

The South Wales Hunts game was won by ten runs, largely thanks to Mike Harrison's four for 47. Earlier Rob Lunn had taken 65 minutes to get off the mark before he was ultimately dismissed for 4 in an OHJ total of 202. On the following day Nick Creed took four for 33 and Mark Semmence four for 16 as the Old Rossallians were bowled out for 152. A 75-run opening partnership between James Larman and Mike Bailey saw the OHJs to an eventual four-wicket victory.

The match against the Cryptics is notorious for the large number of extras conceded by both sides – 53 in the Cryptics innings and 46 in the OHJ innings. The combined total of 99 extras amounted to 18.97% of the 522-run match aggregate. The Cryptics declared at 276 for 7 with S Halliday making 91 and Rutherford 66. In their quest for victory the OHJs began well. Nick Creed made 45 and Mark Semmence 56, but the lower order failed and losing their last wicket off the second ball of the last over, the OHJs were all out for 246.

Mike Harrison took five for 66 against the Stoics who were 99 for 6 at lunch but an early afternoon rally headed by J Kumar, who made 66, led to a Stoics declaration at 236 for 9. In reply the OHJs reached 20 without loss but collapsed to 44 for 7 which soon became 58 for 8. Dick Smart then arrived at the crease to join Mike Harrison. They added 104 runs for the 8th wicket at which point Smart was out for 46. Jeremy Rawlins with 8 * then helped Harrison add a further ten runs before the match ended in a draw with Harrison 56*.

Rain delayed the start of the game against the Sussex Martlets. Ed Welch made 61 in an OHJ total of 181 for 8 declared. In reply the Martlets made 158 for 8 with Paul Hess, the College Chaplain, scoring an aggressive 58 described by George Hill as 'the Church Militant at work'.

Further rain caused the cancellation of the Buccaneers

match and the Week came to a damp end. Nevertheless, there were plenty of players available and the number camping on Manyweathers continued to grow. George Hill concluded his report for the Newsletter as follows:

> Finally thank you to Maurice Pitcher without whom there would probably be no Cricket Week. Was it he who visited us in the guise of a white bird who hovered over and on the North Field for several days during yet another enjoyable visit to Hurst?

2003 was a hot and dry summer with the Week itself, described by George Hill as 'the best cricket week we have had for many years'. He described the weather as 'absolutely wonderful' as the Week unfolded during one of the hottest periods on record and the scorers resorted to the use of an electric fan in the scorebox. The Week also marked the start of a run of twenty matches without defeat.

On the first day Peter Stock took six for 27 against the Eton Ramblers whose innings of 97 only lasted 23.3 overs. Simon Cross made 41* and Ed Welch 56* as the OHJs raced to a nine wicket win in just 16.2 overs. This was followed by a win against Romany who had declared at 242 for 8 – K Saramatunga 111 and Bill Baxter four for 43. Ed Welch, who made 69, and Stuart Hall had a first wicket partnership of 104 and Mark Semmence made 72* to give the OHJs a four-wicket victory.

All three Harrison brothers, Mike, David and Tom, appeared against the South Wales Hunts who declared at 254 for 5 with David Ricketts making 67, Stevens 50 and Beaverstock 65. The OHJs needed only 44.4 overs to win by seven wickets, thanks to 'a magnificent... almost cruel... innings of 122*' by Mike Harrison. Tom Harrison made 46 and Mark Semmence 50.

The next day was something of an anti-climax as the Old Rossallian match ended in a draw. N Laverty made 74 in a total of 231 for 8 declared. Nick Creed made 75 but it was not enough as the OHJs ended 27 runs short with four wickets in hand. It was altogether different on the Wednesday when the Cryptics were beaten by six wickets.

J Roycroft 65 and R Williams 59 enabled them to declare at 239 for 8. Led by Nick Creed 92, Mark Semmence 62 and Mike Harrison with a quick-fire 42*, the OHJs raced to a six wicket win in just 38.2 overs.

The Stoics were bowled out for 118. Judging by what had happened in the previous matches it was probably expected that there would be another easy victory, but the OHJs found themselves at 26 for 4, then 68 for 5, 83 for 6 and 110 for 7. That they got home in the end was due to Mike Harrison who held things together with an innings of 47.

After 28 years as coach and groundsman Derek Semmence retired and the Sussex Martlets match marked the occasion. A high-scoring match ended in a draw. The OHJs declared at 292 for 3 – Ed Welch 52, Nick Creed 59 and Mark Semmence 113*. In reply the Martlets reached 290 for 9. Derek himself made 85, Martin Speight 57 and Charlie Hartridge 60. The day ended with a Dinner in the College Dining Hall in honour of Derek.

The Buccaneers, with two first-class cricketers – Rob Rydon and S Woolfries - in their ranks as well as Jamie Clifford, who was Kent County Cricket Club Chief Executive before becoming an MCC Assistant Secretary, were all out for 128 after Lee Atkins had taken six for 38. Thanks to Tom Price, 55, and John Goodacre, 54*, the OHJs won by three wickets to end a very memorable Week.

The Week of 2004 was warm and sunny, so it was a pity that Romany were unable to raise a team on the Sunday. On the previous day the Eton Ramblers match had ended in a draw with the OHJs needing to take two more wickets and the Ramblers 50 more runs.

Five consecutive victories followed. The South Wales Hunts made 205 and the OHJs had little difficulty in winning by four wickets. There was another four-wicket win over the Old Rossallians who were dismissed for 198 – S Roberts 56. A responsible 69 from Mike Harrison helped the OHJs to reach the required target with time to spare. The Cryptics were dismissed for 154. Initially the OHJs struggled against the bowling of T McPhail who took five for 38, but sensible batting saw them to a three-wicket win. The Stoics were beaten by 140 runs. Mike Harrison, 53, and John Goodacre, 50*, allowed the OHJs to declare at 221 for 3. The Stoics collapsed for 81 as Nick Creed took four for 33 and Mike Harrison three for 33.

Thanks to the former Sussex player SP Hoadley who made 106*, the Sussex Martlets were able to declare at 201 for 5, but not before there had been considerable excitement. Derek Semmence was dropped on 0 by Guy Mance, who subsequently left for New Zealand. The two events were not connected. This was the nearest Derek had come to joining the Duck Club. The OHJs then won by three wickets with Stuart Hall making 57. The last match of 2004 ended in a draw. The Buccaneers made 276 for 4 before declaring, J Stringer making 74 and N Faber 83. Despite 102 from Mark Semmence the OHJs were only able to reach 196 for 4.

After close of play in time honoured fashion as Dick Smart played the Last Post, George Hill lowered the OHJ flag. He then announced his retirement as Manager of the Week and said that Tom Moulton would be succeeding him. Thus, the second Cricket Week Managership came to an end.

MA Pitcher – founder and the first manager.
[Hurstpierpoint College Archives]

Old Hurst Johnians 1921
Standing (l to r): AJ Russell, RN Lee, EL Pitcher, JH Norton,
FM Bannister, A Goodger, AC Tucker.
Seated (l to r): Rev KG Packard, MA Pitcher, Rev VR Rogers (captain),
DR Baylis, WDC Keeson.
On ground: AW Hurlstone (scorer).
[OHJCC]

The old pavilion.
[Hurstpierpoint College Archives]

The present pavilion.
[John Bettridge]

REV V.R. ROGERS.
O.J. CAPTAIN.

M.A. PITCHER KEEPS THE FIELDERS WARM

M.A.Pitcher viewed from Mid-off

His Excellency
The Umpire
Aug 1921.

*Top left: Rev VR Rogers –
the first captain.*

Top right: MA Pitcher batting

Bottom left: MA Pitcher bowling

*Bottom right: Canon AH Coombes –
Headmaster and Umpire.
[OHJCC]*

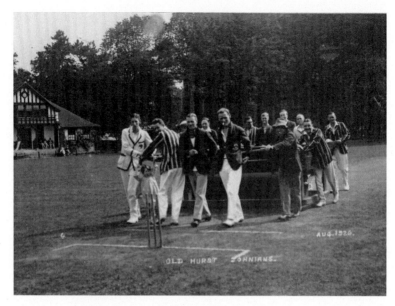

All hands to the roller.
[OHJCC]

Old Hurst Johnians v Sussex Clergy 1924.
The occasion when 13 clergymen took the field.
[OHJCC]

Top left: EL Pitcher. [OHJCC]

Top right: Cricket in the Fleur de Lys Dormitory. [OHJCC]

Bottom left: Jack Youngman. [OHJCC]

Bottom right: After the day's play. [OHJCC]

The record OHJ score.
[OHJCC]

Leo Ricketts.
[OHJCC]

Old Hurst Johnians 1931
Standing, (back l to r): DM Wood, A.C.Tucker, FE Whitbourn, SL Goatly,
FRS Whitbourn, E Bradbrooke, ES Harman. Standing, (front l to r): JE Stevens,
HM Parham, PW Scott, EW Rawkins, CW Thomas. Seated (l to r): DG Jeffery,
DG Mills, MA Pitcher (Manager and Captain), JFA Campbell, CI'A Carr.
On ground: IB Ingall.
[OHJCC]

*CS Dempster (Leicester Ivanhoe and New Zealand) and AES Rippon
(Hampton Wick and Somerset).
[OHJCC]*

*The final ball v Hampton Wick 1935.
[OHJCC]*

Old Hurst Johnians 1949
Standing (l to r): BG Davis, CR Gerrard, DC Hill, DG Jeffery, RC Schad,
JK Rhoden, GM Pitcher, RW Coley, FJ Leaney (umpire).
Seated (l to r): LC Henwood, JG Youngman, CI'A Carr, LEH Ricketts (Captain),
MA Pitcher (Manager), JH Neal, EG Rawkins. On ground, HJ Pitcher (scorer).
[Hurstpierpoint College Archives]

Old Hurst Johnians 1980
Standing (l to r): NA Budge, JC Rawlins, PB Stock, KL Rickard, A Gough,
AJ Stewart, CJ Cowley. Seated (l to r): GM Pitcher, GL Hill (Manager), RW Smart,
WA Welch (Captain), KR Jenkin, ERH Goodacre, JB Goodacre.
[Roger Goodacre]

HURST
JOHNIAN CLUB

NEWSLETTER SUMMER 2006

*Above: The two surviving managers –
George Hill and Tom Moulton in 2006.
[Hurst Johnian Club]*

*Right: 4 August 2014: Tom Moulton
reads the names of the fallen.
[John Bettridge]*

*Bottom: 4 August 2014: the assembled
players and spectators.
[John Bettridge]*

The memorial plaque in the pavilion. [Hurstpierpoint College Archives]

The pavilion and the chapel. [Tom Moulton]

Tea time. [John Bettridge]

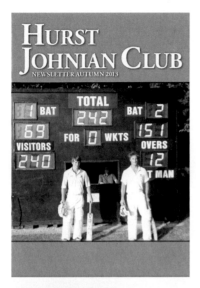

Top: Greg Wisdom and Chris Viggor stand in front of the scorebox at the end of the match against the Stoics in 2013.
[Hurst Johnian Club]

Middle: A formidable panel of experts: (l to r): Willie Welch, Bob Schad, Reg Ruddock, Michael Watkins, Derek Semmence.
[Bruce Ruddock]

Bottom: The shadows lengthen as the Eton Ramblers play out time.
[John Bettridge]

The backdrop of the camp site. [Tom Moulton]

Old Hurst Johnians 2018
Standing (l to r): RStJ Hickman, SJ Warrender (Captain), WV Wild, JE Riddy, MRH Ellis, DG Burstow, R Lunn. Seated (l to r): REL Willsdon, MJ Semmence, SRJ Hall, EW Welch. [Tom Moulton]

Jeremy Rawlins (wicketkeeper), Stuart Hall and Matt Lowndes. [Tom Moulton]

Chapter Six
Tom Moulton 2005 to 2019

As had been the case with the only previous change of managership the transition was seamless, and the Week continued to evolve as it always had done. Tom Moulton was the ideal person to take over. A schoolmaster by profession, he had spent all his formative years on the College campus, had been involved since the age of nine in scoring during the Week and had played his first match in 1986. As was the case with his predecessor, being a teacher meant that he had the time in the summer holidays to spend the best part of a fortnight at Hurst organizing the Week.

The 2005 Week began with a 149-run victory over the Eton Ramblers who arrived with only ten players. Batting first the OHJs declared at 243 for 6 with Mike Harrison having made 83. The Ramblers could only manage a total of 94 with the wickets being shared between the five bowlers, one of whom was Dick Smart who took his 400th wicket in a Cricket Week career stretching back to 1963. The OHJs had to work harder against Romany who made 196, C Grierson 63. Batting was hard going and the OHJs struggled to reach 173 for 9 as Patrick McGahan and Roger Hickman shared an unbroken last wicket stand of 14 to ward off defeat.

2005 was the year that England regained the Ashes: it also marked the Sussex Martlets centenary. Because of their celebrations the match was moved to the Monday, with the South Wales Hunts taking over the Friday slot. In the event heavy rain prevented any play at all. The weather then relented for the Old Rossallian match. The OHJs won a low-scoring game by four wickets, John Goodacre 52, after the Old Rossallians had been dismissed for 119, despite the dropping of six catches.

Joe Ireland took five for 73 for the Cryptics as the OHJs made 227. W McPhail scored 68, but good bowling by Tim

Firth, Deputy Head and an Oxford Blue, who had dismissed Michael Atherton lbw in both innings in the University match of 1987, took four for 56 and the OHJs won by 18 runs.

The sequence of 21 matches without defeat came to an abrupt end when the Stoics were victorious. Put into bat they declared at 297 for 6, J Hatten 56, I Cripps 65 and J Roy 55. The OHJ batting collapsed. Three players failed to score and a further four were dismissed for single figures. The score had reached 82 for 9 when John Saunders, 20*, and Jeremy Rawlins, 27, came together and added 47 for the last wicket before the Stoics won by 168 runs.

On the following day the South Wales Hunts declared at 272 for 7 - Stephens 53, M Clayden 58 and N Morgan 96. M Thomas then took six for 48 as the OHJs were dismissed for 216. The only players to succeed with the bat were Mike Harrison who made 50 and, in the words of the Newsletter report 'to the amazement of all spectators', Patrick McGahan made 46.

The Week ended in exciting fashion with the Buccaneers winning by four wickets with three balls of the last over remaining, J Harcourt having made 101. Previously the OHJs had been dismissed for 228 - Jonathan Pilgrim 61 and Stuart Maddock 65. It will be noted that the other nine batsmen contributed 102 between them.

Tom Moulton ended his report for 2005 with these words:

> Finally, the biggest thank you should go to George Hill for his superb management of Cricket Week between 1973 and 2004, and for his amazing ability to be extremely helpful to the new manager without ever interfering.

The 2006 Week produced a lot of entertaining cricket. Tim Firth had figures of five for 40 as the Eton Ramblers scored 271 for 9 before declaring, Rudd having made 70 and McCall 67. Although Mark Semmence made 75, the OHJs struggled to reach 167 for 9.

Matters were complicated on the Sunday. The OHJs had

made their way to the semi-final of the Brewers' Cup which, because of bad weather, had had to be postponed. It therefore became necessary to put out two teams – one to play Romany and one to play the Old Cranleighans. This stretched the playing resources and unsurprisingly both matches were lost. In the Cricket Week game T Deacon made 101*and Romany declared at 189 for 6. Rupert Hill made 49 but the OHJs were dismissed for 174 as H Corbett took five for 25.

On the following day the South Wales Hunts were defeated by 51 runs. Batting first the OHJs made 230. Although J Richards scored 56, steady bowling saw the Hunts dismissed for 178. On Tuesday Connolly scored 101* for the Old Rossallians who declared at 232 for 5. Ben Searls then made 82 which led to a four-wicket win. The victorious run was maintained on the Wednesday. Tim Firth took four for 30 as the Cryptics were bowled out for 162. Despite the loss of two early wickets consistent batting took the OHJs to a five-wicket victory.

It was more of a struggle on Thursday. H Cripps made 60 as the Stoics recovered from 135 for 7 to 213. The OHJ innings followed a similar pattern: the eighth wicket fell at 148 at which point Harris and Rikki Hill added 56 for the ninth wicket. Rupert Hill then helped his brother take the OHJs to victory. The Sussex Martlets made 190 but, thanks to a splendid 107* by Ben Searls, the OHJs raced to a seven-wicket victory.

The Buccaneers won by 39 runs after declaring at 204 for 8. As had been the case in 1984, the OHJ innings got off to a disastrous start. John Goodacre was dismissed first ball by Urquhart. The next ball was a leg bye which brought Tom Gogarty, in his first and only appearance in the Week, to the striker's end only to be out caught first ball. At the end of the first over the score was 1 for 2. In the next over Rupert Hill was caught off the bowling of Bray: the total was now 1 for 3. The score made its way to 33 for 6 at which point Tim Jarvis and Max McGahan added 55. Jarvis continued to attack the bowling and was eventually out for

93 and the total was 165, Urquhart having taken four for 27.

The weather in 2007 was generally poor. Fortunately, however, the Week turned out to be the only dry one of the summer and all the matches ran their full course.

At lunch on the first day the Eton Ramblers were 89 for 7 with Mike Harrison having taken five for 35 in 13 overs, but an afternoon recovery led by R Briscoe, 78, and Evans, 62, who added 101 for the eighth wicket took the score to 221. Mark Semmence made 91 but had little or no support and the OHJs had reached 177 for 9 by the close. In true Duck Club Presidential style, Bill Baxter held out for forty minutes for 0* while Fergus Boyd took six for 45.

Put into bat Romany declared at 234 for 9, M Corbett having made 102. The OHJs eventually lost by four runs, but not before Max McGahan had scored 116 in a valiant attempt to reach the required target. On Monday the South Wales Hunts collapsed from 83 for 1 to 136 all out due to good bowling by Harry McGahan, Stuart Hall and Roger Hickman. Tim Jarvis scored 64* as the OHJs won by seven wickets. On the following day Tim Jarvis was again the main architect in an eight-wicket defeat of the Old Rossallians after they had declared at 217 for 8, S Porritt having made 86.

Thanks to Joe Ireland who scored 94, the Cryptics recovered from 55 for 5 to 246. Max McGahan made 50, but the OHJs were always behind the clock and could only reach 210 for 7. The Stoics failed to produce a team so there was no match on the Thursday. On Friday the Sussex Martlets won the toss and made 269 – N Seager 70 and S Murdoch 111, adding 139 for the second wicket. Max McGahan took six for 52 but Lee Atkins had the unfortunate experience of being hit for 32 in his only over. Although Mike Harrison made 77, the OHJs never looked like winning and so the match ended in a draw.

Max McGahan continued his run of success with 113 out of an OHJ total of 233 for 8 declared against the Buccaneers who could only manage 131 of which J Marsh, going in at No.4, made an unbeaten 88 – 67% of the runs scored. D Bray with 16 was the only batsman to get into double figures as Stuart Hall took four for 38. This time Lee Atkins took one for 12 in three overs. This was Dick Smart's last Cricket Week appearance. He had made his debut in 1963, had appeared in 227 matches in which he had bowled 3028 overs, more or less all up the hill, taken 403 wickets, 88 catches and scored 1615 runs. He is also only one of two players – Bill Baxter is the other – to have played during all three managerships.

The weather during the 2008 Week was generally reckoned to have been the worst since 1985. Fortunately, there were no cancellations but there were five late starts and one match had to be abandoned.

The Eton Ramblers match started at 1.30 pm. Thanks to 50 from Strang-Steel and 59 from A Rudd before he had to retire hurt, the Ramblers declared at 220 for 4. The OHJs collapsed to 82 for 5. Mike Harrison, 86, and Stuart Hall, 57, added 102 for the seventh wicket, but the last three wickets could only manage another 9 runs which took the total to 193. T McCall took five for 69. On Sunday play was abandoned at 5.30 pm with the OHJs on 54 for 2 needing another 104 to beat Romany.

The weather was better on Monday. The South Wales Hunts made 207 – J Marsh 55*, but M Thomas took six for 21 as the OHJs were all out for 120. More rain led to a late start to the Old Rossallian match and it was agreed to have 40 overs each. The match was dominated by LA Dingle who made 80 out of 156 for 7. Needing 158 the OHJs reached 117 for 5, Jack Riddy having made 52, but Dingle then took five wickets in 12 balls, a spell which included four wickets in six balls, and the Old Rossallians won by 16 runs.

The Cryptics match was a tame draw. The OHJs made 213, Mark Semmence 61, which took 50.5 overs. The Cryptics lost early wickets and were 22 for 4. A Scott, 102*, and A Hall added 119 for the sixth wicket, but even so the total had only reached 169 for 6 in 50 overs when close of play came. On Thursday the Stoics declared at 244 for 7 – A

Wales 74. The OHJs had staggered to 74 for 6 when Stuart Hall, 53, and Patrick McGahan, 46, joined forces. The score rose to 192 for 7 which soon became 192 for 8. A further run was added, and the match ended in a draw.

Another collapse occurred in the Sussex Martlets match. Put in to bat the Martlets made 221 for 2 declared with S Carter making 81 and RO Allum 85 in a first-wicket partnership of 135. In reply Tom Harrison made 72, but the last five OHJ wickets fell for 14 runs and the match was lost by 29 runs.

The Buccaneers match was played in dreadful weather, the players being off the field for most of the time between lunch and tea. Before that the Buccaneers had made 160 for 2 thanks to a partnership of 123 by K Ross 77 and J Mann 58*. They then declared and in extremely bad conditions, especially for the fielders, umpires and scorers, Greg Haines 65* and Tom Harrison 88* took the OHJs to a somewhat unsatisfactory 10 wicket win.

The weather in 2009 was not a great deal better. The Eton Ramblers match was abandoned because of rain with the Ramblers on 136 for 7. Sunday was brighter. Romany were dismissed for 136 which would have been less had not the 9th wicket added 20 and the 10th 31. The OHJs then contrived to lose eight wickets – Charles Fellows-Smith four for 39 – before they won.

On Monday J Lawlor made 73 as the South Wales Hunts reached 245 with Max McGahan taking five for 58. Although Mike Harrison made 70, the OHJs could not score quickly enough only managing 186 for 7. The Old Rossallians dismissed the OHJs for 119 and went on to win by four wickets.

On Wednesday Max McGahan was again amongst the wickets, taking five for 68, as the Cryptics were dismissed for 173.The OHJs won by four wickets with Nick Creed making 51*. The OHJ task would have been easier had it not been for a tenth wicket partnership of 38 between C Fox and William Buckland, author of the cricket polemic *Pommies* which had recently been short-listed for the MCC/

Cricket Society Book of the Year award. The rain returned to bring the Stoics match to a premature end. The OHJs were 80 for 6 in reply to the Stoics total of 214, H Cripps 78.

On Friday Mike Harrison made an unbeaten 77 as the OHJs made 199 against the Sussex Martlets whose reply began in spectacular fashion when Mike Harrison had Derek Semmence lbw for 0 and who therefore at long last joined the Duck Club. So long had been the wait and so unexpected was the dismissal that the event – much to the bowler's lasting dismay – was greeted with almost minimal applause. J Maxwell made 50 as the Martlets were dismissed for 122.

Good bowling, especially by Stuart Hall whose figures of 8-8-0-4 (statistically the best OHJ bowling figures of all time), led to the dismissal of the Buccaneers for 106. Led by Bill Baxter with an aggressive 36*, the OHJs were victorious by six wickets.

The weather in 2010 was better, but even so the rain brought two matches to a standstill. The Eton Ramblers match ended at 5.00 pm with the OHJs victorious by six wickets having only needed 122 to win. Tom Harrison made 66. In what was the most exciting game of the Week, Romany were defeated by two wickets. Romany declared at 200 for 7, M Corbett 56. Led by Simon May with 54, the OHJs looked on course for a comfortable win but, having reached 150 for 3, there was a mini-collapse and it was the ninth wicket pair of Danny Burstow and Mark Ellis that saw the OHJs to a two-wicket victory.

The South Wales Hunts could only manage 109 and the OHJs won easily by eight wickets with Chris Viggor unbeaten on 50. On the Tuesday Mike Harrison took five for 41 as the Old Rossallians were dismissed for 115. The OHJs struggled to 79 for 5 at which point Nick Creed and Bill Baxter came together in a sixth wicket partnership to win the match.

Early afternoon rain caused the abandonment of the Cryptics match when the OHJs had made 195 for 4 with Tom Harrison on 71. Thursday was a blank day as once again the Stoics failed to produce a team. Further rain affected the Sussex Martlets match but not before the OHJs had made 271 for 5 declared. Mike Harrison made an unbeaten 100, having broken a car window and hit the Chapel wall with a straight six, very probably similar to the six sixes, two which were very close to the chapel windows, hit by Patsy Hendren in his pre-lunch innings of 154 for the MCC against the College in 1912. Mike's younger brother Tom had made 58. By the time the rain came the Sussex Martlets were 124 for 5 – S Carter 57. All five had been taken by Mike Harrison – five for 31.

One of the drawbacks of the electronic scoreboard has been that it does not show when the last wicket fell. This shortcoming was very apparent in the match against the Buccaneers. The Buccaneers collapsed to 110 for 9 when Rob Rydon was joined by W Okines. They had added 98 for the tenth wicket – Rydon 87* and Okines 22* and had no means of knowing how much they had put on – when Rydon declared. Needing 209 the OHJs won by seven wickets thanks to a 'sublime' 95 from Will Wild and 62 from Mike Harrison.

Despite the fact that the Romany and Stoics matches had for different reasons to be cancelled the Week of 2011 was as enjoyable as ever. Wickets were hard to come by and only twice did a team lose all ten wickets. 3,114 runs were scored in the six matches for the loss of 73 wickets – a cost 42.66 runs per wicket.

The match against the Eton Ramblers was, on the one hand a statistician's delight but, on the other hand, a bowler's nightmare. The match aggregate was 649 for 6 scored in 88.1 overs. The OHJs batted first. Tom Harrison made 53, Chris Viggor 86, Ed Welch 103 and the OHJs declared at 323 for 3. The Ramblers were soon 3 for 1, but Tim McCall set about the bowling, carting it to all corners of the North Field and running the fielders ragged. Bill Baxter suffered the indignity of being hit for 34 (five sixes and one four) in one over and having the unenviable figures of 2-0-47-0. McCall's score was 242* when the Ramblers won by seven wickets. This is the highest score made in the Cricket Week, beating Jack Youngman's 191* in 1934, the highest score made against the OHJs and it is also the ground record.

The Romany game was called off because of a number of logistical problems brought about by the fact that the OHJs were due to play at home in the semi-final of the Brewers' Cup against Old King's Scholars. This match was won and the OHJs moved on to the final.

The match against the South Wales Hunts was drawn but there were only three runs in it at the end. Thanks to Rhys Morgan with an unbeaten 100 and 67 from T Sidford, the Hunts were able to declare at 268 for 3. Although Mark Semmence made 86 and Tudor Carr 57*, the OHJs, in that awful sporting cliché, 'could not quite get over the line'. The Old Rossallian match was a high-scoring draw. The OHJs declared at 314 for 4, Mark Semmence 69, Nick Creed 82 and Mike Harrison 92. The Old Rossallians made 273 for 5 – C Preston 58, T Facer 55 and RA Dingle 68*.

Runs were harder to come by on the Wednesday when the Cryptics won by three wickets. Joe Ireland took five for 20 in the dismissal of the OHJs for 181 – Josh Menzies top-scoring with 59*. Although Rob Noble took five for 64, the Cryptics won by 3 wickets with their innings held together by an unbeaten 93 from J Doole. Rain then led to the cancellation of the Stoics match. The Sussex Martlets won by 19 runs after they had declared at 257 for 9 and A Davies had scored 126. In reply Tudor Carr made 101, but there was not enough support and the OHJs were all out for 238.

The Week ended with a memorable victory over the Buccaneers. The OHJs had considerable selection problems which led to the Manager and his 13-year-old son having to play. At least three of the team had injuries and really should not have played. The batting was fairly strong, but the bowling resources were thin. In the event, captained by Matt Lowndes, the OHJs batted first and declared at 263 for 3 – Mark Semmence 127* and Tom Harrison 62. The threadbare OHJ attack rose to the occasion. Chris Viggor, a part-time seamer, took five for 73, the schoolboy Joe Woods three for 53 with the other two wickets being taken by father and son Moulton. All the catches went to the best fielders and the Buccaneers were all out for 222.

2012 was one of the wettest summers for many years so it was remarkable that all eight games were completed. In a match which should be called Baxter's Revenge, the Eton Ramblers were defeated by 191 runs – a complete change from the previous year's OHJ failure to defend a total of 323 for 3 declared. An innings of 123 from Tom Harrison who shared a fifth wicket partnership of 143 with Seb Broster led to a declaration at 281 for 8. The Ramblers collapsed for 90. Tim McCall, the hero of the previous year's match, was dismissed by Stuart Hall for 19. The wickets were shared by the spinners – Stuart Hall four for 26, Ben Moulton three for 12 and Bill Baxter three for 12.

On Sunday Romany recovered from 36 for 4 to 240 for 7 – T Deacon 83 and M Corbett 97*. The OHJs began well, reaching 152 for 2 with the last twenty overs yet to start but there were then two run outs in two balls. Tom Moulton's report continues:

> The game was eventually drawn in comic style with number 11 Josh Menzies – 2* – blocking resolutely at one end and Patrick McGahan slogging wildly at the other.

The South Wales Hunts won by five runs in the last over after Josh Menzies had taken six for 39 as the Hunts scored 263. The OHJs began well – Nick Creed 66 and Mike Harrison 73 – but the last five wickets could only add 20 more runs as L Burns took five for 86.

Having been 38 for 4, D Green made 69 and the Old Rossallians reached 218 with Ben Moulton taking four for 47. In reply the OHJs collapsed from 93 for 2 to 118 for 7, but Simon Warrender with 80*, aided by Josh Menzies and Tim Thorstensen, held out for a draw. The Cryptics won by 62 runs. J Doole made 50 and Simon Halliday 91 which led to a declaration at 230 for 6. The OHJs were then bowled out for a disappointing 168. In the words of Tom Moulton's report:

> The innings might best be remembered for Nick Chadwell's entertaining 28, in which he changed his headgear twice and was eventually caught behind whilst throwing his bat 20 yards towards fine leg.

Humour is never far away in the Cricket Week.

The Stoics began at a rapid rate and, with fifties from K Stuart 50, AH Davies 61 and CR Davies 50, they declared at 258 for 8. Although Joe Woods scored a rapid 61 and Mark Semmence made 54, the OHJs never scored fast enough and the match petered out into a draw. This was followed by a 151-run victory over the Sussex Martlets. Chris Viggor made 94 and the OHJs declared at 285 for 7. The three spinners, Roger Hickman, Stuart Hall and Joe Woods then bowled out the Martlets for 134.

The Buccaneers declared at 266 for 5 – K Ross 115 and Rob Rydon 58*. In the OHJ reply Will Wild was dismissed with the score at 14. Mark Semmence 125* and Chris Viggor 107 then added 225 for the second wicket to pave the way to an eight-wicket victory.

The report for the 2013 Week began thus:

> This was a wonderful Week in which the most pleasing aspect was the number of young OJs who played. No fewer than twelve people made their Cricket Week debuts... Five 2013 leavers played.

A stronger Eton Rambler side made 302 for 9 – A Ball 115 – and, although Jay Barclay made 79 and Stuart Hall 53*, the Ramblers won by 51 runs. The Romany match ended in a draw after the OHJs had declared at 254 for 5 – Ed Welch 72 and Omkar Khot 62*. Romany began well – N Angus 78 – but tight bowling by Danny Burstow – one for 19 in 11 overs – and an impressive five for 34 by Barclay, almost brought victory as Romany ended on 200 for 8.

The South Wales Hunts made 238 for 6 declared with Dave Ricketts again in the runs with 99. The OHJs had reached 26 for 2 when the rain came. On the following day LCW

Williams took seven for 29 as the OHJs collapsed for 145. The Old Rossallians only needed 22 overs to win by four wickets. After Mark Semmence had made 114* off the Cryptics bowling, the OHJs declared at 205 for 8. With only ten men the Cryptics were bowled out for 143, thus losing by 62 runs.

The Stoics match provided one of the most memorable victories in OHJ cricket. S Campbell made 126 and the Stoics declared at 240 for 6 which they must have thought was a competitive score, but 36.1 overs later they had lost by 10 wickets. Chris Viggor, knocking up an incredible and at times brutal 151*, and Greg Wisdom making 69*, broke all the partnership records in the history of OHJ cricket. The partnership is probably a ground record and it is unlikely that any higher score has been made at Hurst to win a match by ten wickets.

Friday's game was a quieter affair as the Sussex Martlets were beaten by five wickets after being dismissed for 154 – S Scott 57. After the previous day's heroics Chris Viggor was out for 1, but Mark Semmence 67 and Brad Gayler 50* took the OHJs to victory. On Saturday Simon Warrender declared with the OHJ total at 290 for 5. He had made 80, Stuart Hall 78 and Mike Harrison 50. This looked like a defendable total but M Ragnauth, a Cambridge blue and one of three first-class cricketers in the Buccaneers team, made 137 and the Buccaneers won by three wickets to end what had been a memorable Week.

The 2014 Week was another good one with 38 players available of whom eight were either 2013 or 2014 leavers.

The Eton Ramblers match began well. Mark Semmence made 133* and a total of 253 for 6 declared looked safe enough especially as the Ramblers were soon 53 for 4. Wanting to make a game of it the OHJs opened things up too much with the upshot that the Ramblers only losing one more wicket won by five wickets with J Segall making 55 and T Hawke 118*. On the following day Romany could only manage 128 and the OHJs had a comfortable seven wicket win.

Monday 4 August marked the 100th anniversary of the start of the First World War. At 11.30 am a short Act of Remembrance was held in front of the pavilion. With both the OHJ and South Wales Hunts teams lined up in their whites and quite a sizeable crowd it was a poignant moment in the life of the College, the Hurst Johnian Club and the Old Hurst Johnian Cricket Club. Tom Moulton spoke these words:

> As we stand here today, 100 years after the start of the Great War, it is appropriate to consider the impact that that conflict had on the College and in particular its cricketers. The link between the war and Hurst cricket is clear. This pavilion is the College's memorial to 108 Old Boys who lost their lives, with the clock dedicated to the memory of four masters who died, including the master i/c of cricket. The Cricket Week itself, founded in 1920, clearly had the shadow of the war hanging over it. Five of those who played in the 1914 XI were killed whilst the nine survivors all played in the Cricket Week in the 1920s with five of the team playing in the inaugural Week.
>
> In all, 20 OJs who played cricket in the 1st XI were killed.
>
> Let us remember them by name and then hold a minute's silence in recognition of their sacrifice.
>
> > They shall grow not old as we that are left grow old.
> > Age will not weary them, nor the years condemn.
> > At the going down of the sun and in the morning, we shall remember them.

Moments later the match began. The Hunts could only manage 201 runs in 56 overs, but the OHJs struggled against the bowling of L Burns who took five for 35 and lost by 59 runs.

It was a different story on the following day. The OHJs declared at 237 for 3 with Simon Warrender scoring 110* and Andy Jenks 60. Greg Wisdom then tore through the Old Rossallian batting, taking seven for 29 in a 71-run victory with only LCW Williams 57 and Jonty Arundel 70* providing any resistance.

On Wednesday the OHJs declared at 252 for 5 against the Cryptics. Will Wild scored 100 and Mike Harrison 65. Despite the efforts of Jamie Hutchings – four for 36 – and an attempt to open up the game the Cryptics showed no interest in going for the runs. Omkar Khot bowled six overs – all of them maidens and Bill Baxter only conceded 19 runs in five overs as the game was left drawn.

The Stoics arrived on Thursday and took their first OHJ wicket since 2012. Greg Wisdom scored 110 and the OHJs declared at 267 for 4. The Stoics began well – A Clark 75 and I Harvey 78 put on 143 for the first wicket. Aided by good catching the OHJ spinners then took control, and with Omkar Khot taking four for 64, Matthew Isepp 2 for 47 and Ben Moulton three for 17, the game was won by 72 runs.

On the following day against the Sussex Martlets, Marcus Campopiano, 131, Joe Ludlow, who still had a year to go at school, with 64, and Mike Harrison making a typical late assault on the bowling, 55*, meant that the OHJs were able to declare at 303 for 5. Good bowling by Jamie Hutchings, four for 30, and Stuart Hall, four for 13, took the OHJs to a 105 run victory.

During the tea interval of the match against the Buccaneers which they won by three wickets – JG Milne 59 and Roger Hickman four for 28 having dismissed the OHJs for 197, Yvonne Rose presented a cup to be won by the person who made a difference in the Week in memory of her husband Martin who had died of cancer earlier in the year. Martin had made many contributions to OHJ cricket, in particular skippering the OHJ touring side to Barbados in 1987 and leading the OHJs to victory in the Brewers' Cup Final in 1988.

2015 was a batsman's Week. In seven matches – the Cryptics were unable to raise a side – 3567 runs were scored at an average cost per wicket of 38.77. It was definitely the wrong Week to take up bowling.

The Week began with a victory against the Eton Ramblers. The OHJs declared at 258 for 7 with Mark Semmence having made 123. Despite a ninth wicket partnership of 100 by Forbes and T Hawke, the Ramblers lost by 30 runs. Romany were defeated by 88 runs in a match notable for the fact that there were three individual scores of 46.

The really high scoring began on Monday against the South Wales Hunts. The OHJs declared at 292 for 7 – Will Wild 82 and Joe Ludlow 111. The Hunts replied with 295 for 2 at a scoring rate of 6.2 runs per over. A Davies 123* and J Davies 111* had an unfinished partnership of 226 and the match was won with seven of the final twenty overs remaining.

Scoring at 6.02 runs per over the Old Rossallians declared at 333 for 5 – R Price Moore 66 and B Johnston 139. Led by Marcus Campopiano 102, Greg Wisdom 52 and Joe Ludlow 150*, the OHJs, scoring at a rate 6.67, won by seven wickets in just 49.4 overs. The match aggregate was 667 for 8.

One can only imagine what might have happened had the Cryptics been able to raise a side as the run spree continued in the Stoics match on Thursday. Batting first the OHJs declared at 300 for 3. After Will Wild had made 52, Joe Ludlow 103 and Mark Semmence 102*added 213 for the third wicket. The Stoics then proceeded to win by eight wickets. D Graycon, 99, and O Smith, 150, scoring at 6.91 runs per over, put on 252 for the first wicket. Victory came in just 44.1 overs.

Having scored three consecutive centuries Joe Ludlow was unavailable for the match against the Sussex Martlets who, scoring at 8.05 runs per over, declared at 354 for 4 with SP Cooper making 205* – the second highest individual Cricket Week score. It might have been expected that the OHJs would knock off the runs, but no one made very much and the OHJs were all out for 143.

The Buccaneers match was altogether different. The scoring rate was more normal as the Buccaneers made their way to 219. In reply only Matt Lowndes with a stoical 31 put up much resistance as the Week ended with a 69-

run defeat.

The Week of 2016 was notable for the number of young players. Thirteen of the thirty-eight were aged 22 or under. This meant that there were not only a lot of able and active fielders, but also that there were many who were playing regularly throughout the season.

The Eton Ramblers were beaten by one run. Mike Harrison made 53 out of an OHJ total of 213 and Will Wild joined the Duck Club without anyone noticing. In a typical Cricket Week finish the Ramblers almost won only to lose by one run when Mike Harrison took the last wicket with the last ball of the last possible over.

Romany were beaten by 123 runs. Batting first the OHJs declared at 267 for 4, James Wilkes-Green making 123* and taking part in a 156-run partnership with Simon Warrender 54. James Brehaut, on debut and in the Lower VI, then took four for 36 as Romany were dismissed for 144 with A James scoring 52.

Rain affected the next three days. The South Wales Hunts match ended when the OHJs, needing 224, had reached 29 for 1. By the following morning the North Field was under water and so the Old Rossallian game had to be cancelled and the start of the Cryptics match delayed until 2.00 pm when regrettably and, as it turned out, quite unnecessarily, the captains agreed to a limited overs match – 40 overs each. The OHJs made 218 for 9 in their 40 overs with Brad Gayler making 59. Using six bowlers the Cryptics were then dispatched for 66 in just 19.5 overs.

Matters returned to normal on the Thursday when the Stoics declared at 235 for 5 with D Sear, 96*, and A Jordan, 73. Tim Moses, later a Cambridge blue, made 113, but had little or no support as Paul Meader took six for 30 – including four wickets in seven balls – which gave the Stoics a 29-run win.

On Friday the Sussex Martlets 'batted first and constructed a most extraordinary innings.' Thanks to James Brehaut, who took five for 74, the Martlets were 50 for 5 and then 96 for 6. Then BJP Davies, batting at No.7, launched an all-out assault on the OHJ bowling. By the luncheon adjournment he was 92*. Continuing in like manner after the interval he was eventually dismissed for 171 out of a total of 289 – 66.54% of the runs scored off the bat. Krishana Singh, who had appeared for Loughborough University, made 60, but no one else did a great deal as the OHJs lost by 106 runs in a match in which Rob Willsdon, dismissed first ball of the innings, qualified for membership of the Duck Club in three categories – Caesarean, Adolescent and Premature. Nigel Beacham also joined the Duck Club, although not having appeared in the Week for 20 years he took a wicket with his first ball.

On Saturday J Goodman made 106 for the Buccaneers who declared at 251 for 7. In reply Stuart Hall made 57 but he had little support and the OHJs lost by 187 runs. It is sad but necessary to report that Rob Willsdon failed to score again, thus increasing his total of duck categories to six. This time it was a Duckling, an Adult and a Brood.

During the tea interval in the match against the South Wales Hunts a tree was planted in memory of Hollie Rawlins who, sadly, had died earlier in the year at the age of 30. The daughter of Jeremy and Sarah Rawlins, she had regularly attended the Week with her parents and was very much a part of the whole Cricket Week set-up. She has been very much missed and the tree is a reminder of a most attractive personality.

Thirty-four players were available in 2017 when the weather was variable, but only one match was ruined by rain. The Eton Ramblers match was a good one which built up to an exciting finish. Thanks to Tom and Mike Harrison – 57 and 94 respectively – the total reached 202. The Ramblers were reduced to 96 for 8 but 20 was added for the ninth wicket before the last pair held out for a draw.

Romany were unable to raise a side and there was insufficient notice to arrange an alternative fixture, so everyone had a day off. Some remained on the camp site, while others played for the Sussex Martlets against the

Old Georgians at Weybridge or for the South Wales Hunts against the Guards at Burtons Court. Others watched the Cricketer Cup Final between the Old Eastbournians and the Old Wellingtonians at Arundel.

On Monday the South Wales Hunts collapsed for 101 and were very soon beaten by seven wickets. So soon in fact that there was time for a 20 over match. It would perhaps have been much better to have turned the original match into a four innings game. The Old Rossallian match was drawn. Set 224 to win, the OHJs found themselves fighting off defeat at the close of play – 23 runs short and one wicket in hand. On the following day heavy rain after three-quarters of an hour's play brought the Cryptics match to an abrupt end.

On Thursday the Stoics were put in to bat and, although A Jordan made 51, they were dismissed for 133 with Omkar Khot taking five for 46 and Danny Burstow four for 19. In reply the OHJs were soon 23 for 2 – one of those dismissed being Peter Gann who, having left the College in 1978 and playing in his first-ever Cricket Week game, took one ball to join the Duck Club. Greg Wisdom 46 and Mark Semmence 58 then took the score to 123 before Wisdom was out for 46. Semmence soon followed with the score unchanged. Simon May also left at 123 before Simon Warrender scored 4 only to be out caught – 127 for 6. Ben Moulton scored a single, but Patrick McGahan was quickly dismissed. Omkar Khot arrived and the score reached 129. The Stoics captain brought the field in, but Ben Moulton settled matters with a six onto the bank.

On the following day the Sussex Martlets declared at 258 for 8, N Moller having made 83. Shortly after the OHJ innings began it appeared that there was some confusion over the time for the start of the last 20 overs. To the onlooker this seemed most strange as ever since the requirement that a minimum of 20 overs should be bowled in the last hour became mandatory in all Cricket Week matches 20 overs have always been called at 6.00 pm. After some on-field discussion between the umpires the captains and the

Manager, the last 20 were called – erroneously it has to be said – at 5.30 pm.

Having lost half an hour's batting time, the OHJ batsmen set about the Sussex Martlets bowling in no uncertain manner. In the words of Tom Moulton's report:

> ... we managed to win by 7 wickets in a thrilling run chase. Significant contributions from all the batsmen helped in this. An opening partnership of 65 between Simon Warrender (40) and May (74), was followed by one of 105 between the latter and Joseph Gilligan (63). Simon's clinical pulling and driving was a delight for spectators and it was clear that Joseph Gilligan is a batsman of high quality who has the ability to dismantle a bowling attack with some brutality. Following their display, the fourth wicket pair of James Wilkes-Green (39*) and Ben Moulton (30*) added the remaining 67 runs in 45 balls as the OHJs won with four balls to spare.

The Buccaneers turned up with a side drawn from three families – five Rydons, three Manns and three Milnes. They reached 183 – J Milne 50 and Stuart Hall five for 42 which, most surprisingly, was his first Cricket Week five-wicket haul. In a tight finish the OHJs lost by 5 runs despite a valiant 51* from Simon Warrender.

The summer of 2018 was dry and hot, and these conditions prevailed at the start of the Week. On Saturday the Eton Ramblers declared at 305 for 8 – P Eckersley 120 and Stuart Hall six for 64. The OHJs struggled to 176 for 8. On the following day Stuart Hall took seven for 48 as Romany, in what turned out to be their last appearance in the Week, were dismissed for 200. The OHJs won by nine wickets with all three who got to the wicket scoring fifties – Chris Viggor 50, Tom Harrison 95* and Mark Semmence 54*.

Consistent OHJ batting produced a total of 270 for 8 declared against the South Wales Hunts who, in reply, reached 181 for 2 before collapsing to 221 for 8. T Sidford and Omkar Khot then got together and saw them home to a two-wicket win. This was Canon Bruce Ruddock's first Cricket Week match as umpire and he thus became the second Canon of the Church of England to umpire in Cricket Week after Canon Coombes had done so in 1921.

On Tuesday there was a Great Gathering of Impotent Drakes (or former players) which had been organized by Roger Goodacre. Among those present were Bob Schad, Michael Watkins, Keith Jenkin, George Hill, Robin Carr, Willie Welch, Dick Smart, Hugh Thomas and many others. It was therefore appropriate that the OHJs defeated the Old Rossallians by seven wickets. James Brehaut took six for 47 as the Old Rossallians struggled to 198 – LCW Williams making 92. Two excellent debuts by Tom and Ed Fairfax – 82* and 53 respectively – took the OHJs to victory.

On Wednesday the Cryptics were bowled out for 153 – James Brehaut four for 23 and Stuart Hall four for 47. What followed was one of the more embarrassing OHJ batting displays of recent times as, despite 56 from Tom Fairfax, the OHJs managed to lose by six runs. V Naryan took six for 36 while spectators 'looked on in open-mouthed horror as experienced cricketers inexplicably threw their wickets away.'

Rain then arrived and no play was possible for the next two days. It did not matter much on the Thursday as the Stoics had been unable to raise a team, but Friday was a different matter. After a late start on Saturday the Buccaneers made 254 for 8 declared – J Milne 81 and S Moules 68. Stuart Hall took three for 67 making his haul of wickets for the Week to 20, which was the best since Dick Smart had taken 25 in 1972. Although Simon May made 53 and Mark Semmence 75, the OHJ batting was unable to score fast enough and the match ended in a draw.

2019 was another good summer and the weather during the Week – apart from the last day – was extremely pleasant for both player and spectator. Again, plenty of players were available and it was encouraging to see a number of recent leavers in action.

Overshadowing all this, however, had been the deaths

during the previous winter of Sue Hill and Hugh Thomas. Sue was one half of that remarkable partnership which had managed the Week between 1973 and 2004. She brought the family touch to the Week which, as we have seen, had been an all-male affair in its first fifty years. Sue was the organiser of the match day teas which were enjoyed not only by the players and officials but also the many children who always seemed to know, despite the arcane tea interval regulations, when it was teatime. Appropriately a tree was planted in her memory at the tea interval in the match against the Old Rossallians.

During the luncheon adjournment in the Free Foresters match a tree had been planted in memory of Hugh Thomas. Co-founder with George Pitcher of the daily pre-lunch sherry session, Hugh joined the College staff in 1968 and from then onwards was a great supporter of OHJ cricket as player, umpire and sage spectator. Hugh also accompanied the two OHJ tours to India carrying out his umpiring duties in his usual highly efficient manner.

It was also Neil Sayers' last Cricket Week after 49 years on the College ground staff. Starting as an assistant to David Gibson in 1971, Neil devoted the whole of his working life to the College. A great friend to many OHJs and very much part of the College furniture he will be sorely missed.

On Saturday the OHJs batted for 47 overs against the Eton Ramblers and declared at 294 for 4. Mark Semmence made 121 and Simon Warrender an unbeaten 79. The Ramblers replied with 250 – L Adair 50 and Dan Burstow taking four for 39. It is perhaps somewhat embarrassing to report that Extras amounted to 50. After a gap of 31 years the Free Foresters returned to the Week. The OHJs declared at 254 for 7 – Mark Semmence 83 – but 107 from T Shaw took the Free Foresters to a six wicket victory. This time there were only ten extras.

On Monday Greg Wisdom took six for 66 to help dismiss the South Wales Hunts, fresh from a victory over the Guards the previous day, for 194 – T Sidford 51*. T. Shams then scored 80 as the OHJs raced to a five wicket victory in just 31 overs. For the first time in the history of the Week the OHJs were awarded five penalty runs when the ball hit a helmet.

The runs flowed freely against the Old Rossallians. 78 from Greg Wisdom, 50 from Jimmy Anyon formerly of Warwickshire, Surrey and Sussex and now on the College staff, and 61* by Ben Moulton who took 20 off the over before the declaration, took the OHJ total to 318 for 6. Good OHJ bowling then dismissed the Old Rossallians for 171.

The Cryptics came on Wednesday and with scores of 57 from B Caidan and 78 from James Brehaut, the OHJs were able to reach 236 while Joe Ireland took five for 82 in 21 overs. The Cryptics lost quick wickets and at the start of the last hour were 90 for 8. Good defensive play by J Hamilton 55* and P Armstrong held out for another 12.4 overs. Hamilton was then joined by Will Buckland who were both still there at the close.

There were two notable occurrences in this match. For the second time in three matches the OHJs were awarded five penalty runs because the ball hit a helmet. Perhaps even more extraordinary was the fact that 22 overs were bowled between 6.00 and 7.00 – a most unusual event in 21st century cricket.

On Thursday the Stoics won by seven wickets. Batting first the OHJs subsided to 92 for 6. James Brehaut, 64, and Matt Isepp, 53, then added 101 and the total eventually reached 242 with J Smith having taken five for 33. The Stoics lost a quick wicket but then D Sear, 88, and D Rippingdale, 134, added 220 for the second wicket and the Stoics galloped to victory by seven wickets. On the following day the Sussex Martlets declared at 278 for 7 – T Shepperton (a current College pupil) 101*, and J Willoughby, 73. The OHJs were never in the hunt. Wickets fell steadily and only Leo Cammish, a Sussex 2nd XI player, stood firm as he played an impressive innings of 95.

A considerable deterioration in the weather saw heavy

overnight rain followed by high winds. This led to a delayed start against the Buccaneers. Play began at 1.30 pm in the teeth of a very strong south-westerly wind. The Buccaneers declared at 213 for 6 – E Kalidasan having made 51. The OHJs struggled and the last twenty overs began with the total at 91 for 5. This soon became 102 for 8 with 15 overs still left. At this point Dan Burstow joined Rob Noble and they stayed together, adding 50 runs, until Burstow was bowled by the fourth ball of the last over. This brought Patrick McGahan to the wicket. He made one of his traditional swings at the fifth ball and missed, but, fortunately, it passed harmlessly by as did the sixth ball and the match was drawn.

Ten minutes later, as Sam Moulton (standing in for the absent Dick Smart) played the Last Post, Tom Moulton lowered the Old Hurst Johnian flag signifying not only the end of the 2019 Week, but also the fact that the Week had reached the end of its first century.

Chapter Seven
Other Old Hurst Johnian Cricket

It would be a very serious mistake on anyone's part to assume, central though it is, that OHJ cricket is just the Cricket Week. Although the historical record – especially in more recent times – is not as complete as it should be the OHJs have played a lot of other matches.

Since the 1850s the OHJs have played regularly against the College with sometimes as many as three teams. They have taken part in the Brewers' Cup, the Cricketer Trophy, the Cricketer Cup as well as friendly matches against the Common Room and other teams besides making tours to Barbados and India.

The annual match against the College 1st XI is first recorded in the 1858 *Hurst Johnian* and it would appear that, even when the school was less than ten years old, the fixture was already a well-established part of the calendar. With the exception of the wartime seasons of 1915 to 1918 and 1940 to 1945 the match has been played every year. Originally known as Past v Present, it was for many years played at the Whit Bank holiday weekend and was an occasion of considerable importance in the Hurst calendar. With contraction of the Summer Term and the problems caused by the modern exam timetable, the fixture became something of a moveable feast and 2019 most regrettably saw the game being reduced to an afternoon T20 affair which is a far cry from the 1919/1957 period when the OHJs always produced two teams with matches being played on either end of the square.

In 1864 the *Hurst Johnian* published this letter:

London, October 26 1864

Dear Mr Editor,

The half-holiday on Saturday has now become so general that I think that it would be in the power of many of the Old Johnians to join in a friendly game of Cricket during the season. With a view to this, I propose that there should be a Hurst Johnian Club started in London, self-supporting: say the subscription commence at 3s 6d, whilst those who can afford it should pay more; at the end of the season whatever balance there is in hand should be returned to each subscriber according to the amount he pays. If we were fortunate our expenses would amount to little. Of course the first year we cannot expect much.

Leaving it to the better judgment of your readers, and hoping to be called upon to give my mite towards it.

> I remain
> Dear Mr Editor
> Yours truly
> AN OLD 1st ELEVENER

Nothing seems to have come of this suggestion and no other OHJ matches have come to light apart from one against the City of London School in 1914, who were then regular opponents of the College 1st XI, and four appearances in the Bushey Cricket Weeks between 1896 and 1901. The Bushey matches would appear to have come about because of the connection with the Harford family. HM Harford, later to become Captain of Hertfordshire, was at Hurst from 1884 to 1890, being followed by his brother JS from 1895 to 1899. Their father was clearly one of the leading lights of Bushey cricket.

Despite the misgivings of many people cricket at all levels prospered after the First World War. Buoyed by the success of the Week, the OHJs, with MA Pitcher to the fore, began to arrange Saturday fixtures in 1923. At first there was only one match a season with a different opponent being played each time – Old Citizens, Hornsey, Beaconsfield and HAC. In 1929 the fixtures moved to Sundays. Ealing, with whom there was a strong Hurst connection through the Denning family, became annual opponents until the Second World War. This was followed in 1930 by a regular fixture with Hampton Wick which did survive the War. Other opponents included 49 Cricket Club, Shepherd's Bush, South Hampstead, Hornsey, Richmond and the Aladdin Sports Club. In all over forty matches were played and at least four others are known to have been cancelled.

No written accounts of these matches survive but at least the score book does and shows that on occasions sides were made up by a number of ringers – there were five in the Hornsey match of 1939. It also reveals some interesting individual performances. In 1933 Jack Youngman, 101, and Charles Carr, 118, had a first wicket partnership of 210 against Shepherds Bush, amongst whose bowlers was WC Caesar who had played once for Surrey in 1922 and was to appear on three occasions for Somerset in 1946. The OHJ total reached 322 after which Denis Jeffery took seven for 70 as Shepherds Bush were dismissed for 189.

In 1934, CR Crisfield scored 202* out of a Hampton Wick total of 255 for 3 made in 38 overs. In reply the OHJs managed to reach 221. In 1936 the OHJs came up against EA Ingram, a Middlesex and Ireland player, who made 127 out of an Ealing total of 233 for 5 declared. Ingram then took five wickets to seal an Ealing victory. Later that year HF Benka of Middlesex made 75 for Hornsey while PL Worman, a former Lincolnshire player who was then on the College staff and was Housemaster of Red Cross, took four for 50. Later still that season Joe O'Gorman, a Surrey player and the other half of a well-known comedy act with his brother Dave, took six for 46 for Richmond, a feat which he bettered in 1939 when he had figures of seven for 28.

Perhaps the most outstanding feat was that of the Ealing player Robert Felton. An Old Pauline, Felton played occasionally for Middlesex and was better known for his batting, but in 1938 he had figures of six for 14 against the OHJs. In the course of seven overs, two of which were maidens, he achieved the feat of taking four wickets in four balls in his second over and then two in two balls in the fourth. Ealing had two other Middlesex players in action that day – EA Ingram and LB Thompson.

At the Hurst Johnian Club AGM held in January 1933 it was proposed to run an OJ wandering side to play on Saturdays. This was agreed and Max Rhoden was then left to take the proposal forward. An appeal to OHJ cricketers to make themselves available was made in the March issue of the *Hurst Johnian*.

All appears to have proceeded according to plan and in 1934 eighteen matches were played. The majority of the fixtures were in the London area and involved a variety of clubs such as Royal Exchange Assurance, Harrods, Kingston Town and Woodford Green. No scorecards survive, but we are told that Leo Ricketts averaged 48.90 with the bat and that JK Rhoden took 44 wickets at an average of 12.20.

It was reported that a stronger fixture list had been arranged for 1935 but no details are available. Fixture lists for 1936, 1937 and 1938 appear in the *Hurst Johnian* but other information is totally lacking, and no mention is made of anything in 1939. One hopes that research in local newspapers might one day produce something.

The Saturday side went into abeyance during the war. In 1947 it was hoped to revive it. The *Hurst Johnian* recorded the appointment of a committee. It was later reported that a lack of new players and lateness in arranging fixtures had prevented any matches being played. It never was revived and the OHJ fixture list was reduced to the match against the College, an away game against Hampton Wick and, above all, the Week.

In the late 1990s an attempt was made to play some extra fixtures and matches were arranged against the Free Foresters, Old Cranleighans, Lancing Rovers and the HAC. Unfortunately raising sides was not straightforward and the attempt faded away.

One fixture that did endure for over thirty years was a match against the Common Room. This began in 1957 and was last played in the early 1990s. Played on a Sunday towards the end of the Summer Term it was a good social occasion and always attracted plenty of spectators who picnicked around the North Field.

The standard was generally good although on occasion the Common Room side carried a number of passengers who did little more than make up the numbers. There were, however, a number of good performances. In 1962 Jonathan Allison made 52 in an OHJ total of 189 for 6 declared. The Masters lost three quick wickets, but Harry Maxwell, a former Trinity College, Dublin captain with 66*, and Bob Finch, who had played for Berkshire, 90*, added 153 to take the Masters to a seven-wicket victory. A year later Harry Maxwell made 112 out of 223 for 3 declared, but this time the Masters were unable to force a victory.

In a ten-a-side match in 1965 the Masters made 236 of which Robin Gardner, the former Leicestershire player who was the College's coach that year, made 118, sharing a second wicket partnership of 143 with George Hill who made 54. Harry Maxwell then took five for 29 as the OHJs were dismissed for 171, having been 91 for 8. The 1969 game was notable in two ways. Making one of his rare appearances in OHJ cricket Pat Higgs scored 110, but less happy was the experience of Nick Searls, then in his second year of a 37 year teaching career at the College, who was given out lbw to the seventh legitimate ball of the first over for 0.

Following in Robin Gardner's footsteps, in 1971 David Gibson scored a magnificent 135 out of 205 as all around struggled to make any runs at all. Eight years later Bill Baxter distinguished himself by taking five for 34 for the OHJs and then top scoring with 42.

In 1980 Ken Barrington, then a current parent, made a guest appearance for the Masters. Joining the list of Test cricketers who have appeared at Hurst, he made an immaculate 50 before proceeding to give his wicket away. All who met him that day were greatly saddened when he died of a heart attack the following winter when he was Assistant Manager of the England team playing against the

West Indies.

A score card for 1981 survives, but after that the written record is non-existent. One's memory is that the fixture began to decline in popularity, and it is not entirely clear when the last game was played. Despite the revival of Common Room cricket since the turn of the century the fixture against the OHJs has not been restarted.

Between 1973 and 2006 the OHJs took part in the Brewers' Cup. This was a competition which had been set up for schools of 400 or fewer pupils and catered for those old boys' clubs which did not compete for the Cricketer Cup which had been founded in 1967. The OHJs' original opponents were Trent, Denstone, Ellesmere, Bromsgrove, St John's Leatherhead, Dean Close, Prior Park, Oratory, Culford, Aldenham, Bishop's Stortford, Chigwell, Sutton Valence, St Edmund's Canterbury and Seaford.

Although there were some years when raising a side was very difficult, the OHJs won the Cup in 1976, 1978 and 1988 and were runners-up in 1996 and 2004. The semi-final was reached on eight occasions. In all the OHJs took part in 65 Brewers' Cup matches. Unfortunately for the historian only 25 scorecards been found and also the reporting in the Hurst Johnian Newsletter varies from the sparse to the non-existent.

There are, however, a number of anecdotes which have survived. Having won the Cup in 1978 the OHJs found their rain-ruined first round match against Old Seafordians the following year being decided on the toss of a coin. The OHJs lost the toss. On a brighter note in 1981, the OHJs made 238 against the Old Chigwellians and then dismissed them for 98 with Graham Glenn taking five for 9 as they lost their last six wickets for 18 runs.

In 1988 the 58-year-old George Pitcher who, present as a spectator, found himself not only playing in the semi-final against Denstone Wanderers, but also being on the winning side. The Final itself was really a competition between Mark Benson of Kent and England, who scored 80 for the Old Suttonians as they made 245 for 5 in their

55 overs, and Martin Speight of Sussex and Durham, who then made an unbeaten 148 to take the OHJs to a six-wicket victory.

In the First Round in 1993 the Old Aldenhamians made 234. The OHJs reached 233 for 9 with one ball remaining. The nameless OHJ No. 10 was then run out while going for a second run. Had he been successful the OHJs would have won as they had lost one fewer wicket. In 2001 the OHJs reached the semi-final against Old Herefordians only for the game to be washed out, then re-arranged only to be washed out again. It proved to be impossible to raise a team for a third attempt and so the Old Herefordians went through to the Final.

The 2004 Final against the Old Cranleighans was reached after a ten-man OHJ team had beaten the Old Aluredians in the Semi-Final. The Old Cranleighans won off the last possible ball which, sadly, was a no-ball. Two years later the Brewers' Cup came to an end because too many schools were failing to produce teams.

In 2011, however, the Cricketer Trophy began. This was originally competed for by eight old boys' teams. The OHJs won the inaugural tournament when they beat Old Westminsters after a bowl-out, Old King's Scholars and then Denstone Wanderers in the Final. The OHJs reached the Final again in 2015 only to lose heavily to the Old Monmothians in a match played at Gerrards Cross. In mitigation it should be stated that this game came the day after the Week ended.

In 2017 the OHJs were promoted to the Cricketer Cup and began by beating Old Merchant Taylors before losing to the Old Cholmelians. There was a good match against Rugby Meteors in 2018 which was narrowly lost, but the game against Charterhouse Friars in 2019 was one of those occasions when the fates appeared to combine against the OHJs. Jonty Jenner and Tim Moses were playing for Jersey and Cambridge University respectively, George Garton and Tom Haines were required by Sussex while Joe Ludlow and James Brehaut were injured. Little went right in the game itself and Charterhouse Friars, aided by the former Hampshire player James Hamblin, and Olly Batchelor of Leeds/Bradford University, won comfortably by 169 runs.

In April 1987 Alistair Subba Row and Peter Stock organised a two-week tour to Barbados. The party consisted of 17 players, all of whom were OHJs. Ten – Martin Rose, Phil Boddy, Mark and Steve Foulds, Michael Goodall, Justin Graham, Geoff Pike, Andrew Sawers, Mark Speirs and Alistair Subba Row – had toured India with the College side in 1981/82. The rest of the party was made up by John Goodacre, Matt Lowndes, Tom Moulton, Graham Negus, Chris Procter, Peter Stock and Nick Twine.

Accommodated in Worthing on the south coast in self-catering apartments there was ample time to explore the island, enjoy the beaches, sample the nightlife of Bridgetown, and take part in the famous Jolly Roger cruise as well as play cricket. The games were against teams playing in the Barbados Division One Championship and in truth the OHJs were largely outclassed not least because of the strength of West Indian cricket in that era.

Each opposing team had at least two bowlers of terrific pace. Spartan CC began their assault on the OHJ batsmen with an attack which included Ezra Moseley who would go on to break Graham Gooch's hand in the Third Test at Port of Spain in 1989/90. All the matches were 35 overs per side. Usually the OHJs fielded first and usually conceded a sizable total.

Banks Brewery made 278 in 35 overs, during which there were several prolonged intervals as fielders searched for the ball in nearby woodland hoping not to encounter a dangerous or poisonous animal. After conceding large scores the OHJs had to face the firepower of the pace attack. With ten fielders positioned behind square, it was fairly obvious what was coming. Most of the teams bowled their opening pair for their allotted seven overs each, by which time the OHJ total was about 24 for 1, if things were going well, and 24 for 4 if they were not. Either way there were a lot more runs to score in the remaining 21 overs.

Martin Rose, who was in a different class from the rest of the OHJ tourists, coped very well with the fast bowling, but was really the only player to look at all comfortable.

The pitches, which had been soaked, heavily rolled and baked, were raised up from the rest of the playing area. There was not a blade of grass in sight and it was almost possible to see one's reflection in the shiny surface. This was the era when helmets were only just appearing in club and school cricket, so players were generally not used to wearing one. Most of the team soon realised the good sense of taking the precaution, though the sight of the old-school, helmetless, thigh-padless Nick Twine swaying out of the line of a succession of vicious bouncers in the match against the Wanderers, with his family cowering in the pavilion, unable to watch, will remain in the memory of those who were there.

The bowling may have been hostile, but the hospitality off the field was extremely generous. The tourists were often entertained for goat curry and rum punch after a match, and the OHJs were left with the impression that these people, for all the outright hostility of their bowling, were actually wonderfully friendly. There was a victory to savour as well in the last game against the 1987 Barbados Division One Champions – the Police.

Two OHJ tours have been made to India. The first one was in 2000 and included a match at Udaipur, where a ball-by-ball commentary was, provided and a game on the Bombay Maidan where care has to be taken because of all the other games going on at the same time. Hugh Thomas umpired for the OHJs and at the end of the tour he was presented with the Top Tourist Award for his amazing stamina and overall contribution. A second tour, with the party augmented by some invited guests, followed in 2002. This included a game under floodlights in Goa as well as one at the Brabourne Stadium in Bombay. Bangalore and Cochin were also visited. A further tour was planned for 2005 but there were not enough takers and it had to be cancelled.

Conclusion

How has the Week survived to reach its centenary when many other Weeks and indeed Tours are no more? As we have seen the inescapable conclusion must be that the survival and development of the Week is really due to both the enthusiasm of all those who have been involved over the last century and also their ability to cope with and embrace change. What started as a bachelor week has developed into one where wives and families can become involved. The freedom to roam around Manyweathers and the North Field – as long as one does not walk behind the bowler's arm – the 12.30 sherry session, the tea, the general friendly cameraderie amongst those who camp, those who come for the day and, indeed, many of the opposition players who camp overnight, all makes for a perfect and relaxing day at the cricket.

Without players, of course, there could be no cricket and it is a credit to all three managers that there have always been plenty of people willing to play. MA Pitcher began with 14 players in 1920 and, as the College has grown in numbers and now draws many more pupils from Mid-Sussex, Tom Moulton was able to choose from 47 in 2019.

There have, of course, also been changes and developments on the field of play. Totals are higher, more centuries are scored, there are fewer five-wicket hauls and, regrettably, fewer overs are bowled in the day. The quality of play may vary at times, but what never varies is that feeling of enjoyment that one is always aware of when walking round the North Field.

Let George Hill have the last word:

A HEALTH WARNING
Cricket Week is addictive:
once you come, you will come again.

OHJCC Cricket Week Records

Team Records

Highest Total for	370-4	v Rev CH Clarke's XI	1928
Highest Total against	354-4d	by Sussex Martlets	2015
Lowest Total for	39	v Old Colfeians	1922
Lowest Total against	32	by RO Jenkins' XI	1922

Individual Records - Batting

Highest Score for	191*	JG Youngman v WM Bradley's XI	1933
Highest Score against	242*	TP McCall for Eton Ramblers	2011

Individual Records - Bowling

Best Bowling for	9 for 52	JFA Campbell v Rev CH Clarke's XI	1928
	9 for 52	LC Henwood v Stoics	1952
Best Bowling against	10 for 31	SI Rankin for Buccaneers	1973
	10 for 87	AK Wilson for Old Brightonians	1923

Individual Records – Wicket-Keeping

Most dismissals in a match	6 (1/5)	JH Neal v Repton Pilgrims	1959

Career Records

Most appearances	227	RW Smart	1963 - 2007
Most runs in a career	5232	KR Jenkin	1952 - 1991
Most centuries in a career	17	MJ Semmence	1991 - 2019
Most wickets in a career	403	RW Smart	1963 - 2007
Most 5 wickets in a match	22	KR Jenkin	1952 - 1991
Most catches in a career	88	RW Smart	1963 - 2007
Most dismissals by a wicketkeeper			
	165	JC Rawlins (123/42)	1974 - 2015

Week Records

Most runs in a Week	453	A Gough	1984
Most wickets in a Week	27	DG Jeffery	1935
Most catches in a Week	9	WA Welch	1975
Most dismissals in a Week (wk)			
	15 (14/1)	P Hayward	1968

Playing Record

Opponent	Played	Won	Lost	Drawn
Buccaneers	50	20	18	12
Cryptics	46	9	19	18
Eton Ramblers	63	26	19	18
Free Foresters	27	8	10	9
Hampton Wick	16	7	4	5
Leicester Ivanhoe	26	11	8	7
Old Colfeians	14	5	7	2
Old Rossallians	49	16	17	16
Repton Pilgrims	16	2	9	5
Romany	58	29	12	17
South Wales Hunts	29	12	10	7
Stoics	68	28	21	19
Sussex Martlets	86	30	22	34
Sussex Young Amateurs/Cricketers	10	5	4	1
Hove	7	3	1	3
WM Bradley's XI	7	0	5	2
Rev CH Clarke's XI	5	3	1	1
Kingston	4	3	1	0
Old Brightonians	3	0	3	0
Sussex Clergy	3	2	0	1
Haywards Heath	2	1	1	0
HS Mills' XI	2	1	0	1
Old Amplefordians	2	0	0	2
Old Ardinians	2	0	2	0
RAF Cranwell	2	0	2	0
Chichester Priory	1	1	0	0
RJ Coley's XI	1	0	0	1
Cuckfield	1	0	1	0
GE Glenister's XI	1	0	0	1
Hurstpierpoint	1	1	0	0
GM Jeffery's XI	1	1	0	0
RO Jenkins' XI	1	1	0	0
FE Lander's XI	1	0	1	0
Lancing Rovers	1	0	0	1
Mad Hatters	1	1	0	0
Maresfield Camp	1	0	1	0
CW Mills' XI	1	1	0	0
W Riches' XII	1	1	0	0
D Sawer's XI	1	1	0	0
DJ Semmence's XI	1	0	1	0
Total	**612**	**229**	**200**	**183**